Regency Recollections

Captain Gronow's Guide to Life in London and Paris

Edited by Christopher Summerville

❧ • ❧

RAVENHALL BOOKS

Regency Recollections
Captain Gronow's Guide to Life in London and Paris

First published 2006 by Ravenhall Books, an imprint of Linden Publishing l.imited

British Library Cataloguing in Publication Data

Gronow, R. H. (Rees Howell), 1794-1865
Regency recollections : Captain Gronow's guide to life in London and Paris
1.Gronow, R. H. (Rees Howell), 1794-1865
2.Great Britain – Social life and customs – 19th century
I.Title II.Summerville, C. J. (Christopher J.)
941'.073'092

ISBN-10: 1905043074

Ravenhall Books, PO Box 357, Welwyn Garden City, AL6 6WJ, United Kingdom
www.ravenhallbooks.com

Printed and bound in Great Britain
by Creative Print and Design (Wales), Ebbw Vale.

CONTENTS

A picture section appears between pages 96 and 97.

PREFACE

My purpose in presenting this volume of Gronow's celebrated memoirs is to serve up a palatable slice of Regency history for the general reader. To this end, I have strived to prepare a book that is light, pleasing, easily digested, and moreish. There are no lengthy chapters, no dense explanations, and no reams of numbered footnotes. Instead, the reader will, I hope, be pleased to find a platter of anecdotes – Gronow's famous 'souvenirs' – selected, organised, and annotated by myself.

Having described this volume as a history book, I must warn the reader that it contains little in the way of analysis but is, rather, a collection of observations. Here, the details of Regency life are exhibited: how to get invited to a ball, how to fight a duel, how to make a successful elopement, how to win (and just as importantly, how to lose) at the gambling table, how to wear the right trousers. For Gronow was a dandy, and for the dandy, the ultimate triumph is the victory of style over content.

Gronow recorded his reminiscences in the early 1860s, for a Victorian audience eager to learn of the foibles and follies of their parents and grandparents. Living in Paris to avoid debt and writing primarily for the money, Gronow set about remembering – and at times misremembering – the adventures and luminaries of his youth. In his wry and laconic prose we meet the majestically obnoxious Prince Regent, the imperiously mannered 'Beau' Brummell, and the monumentally vain Lord Byron. These celebrities are supported by an endless cast of belles, *beaux sabreurs,* courtesans, dandies, duellists, eccentrics, gamblers, heroes, millionaires, mistresses, matriarchs, and more.

Encouraged by his initial success, Gronow went on to pen four volumes of memoirs, covering the whole period of his life, from the turn of the nineteenth century (he was born in 1794) up to 1865, the year of his death. Despite the occasional lapse of memory – accidental or deliberate – Gronow remains one of the most quoted primary sources on nineteenth-century European history.

There have been several editions of Gronow's memoirs, all of which have sought to offer a random sprinkling of anecdotes from all phases of his life. But the Regency reminiscences are the jewels in Gronow's literary crown, and I hope I have collected the brightest of them in this present volume. I have also sought to arrange these gems in some kind of chronological and thematic order, creating in the process a book of four parts, covering Gronow's experiences in the Peninsular War, at Waterloo, in Restoration Paris and in Regency London.

Other editorial additions include a biographical sketch of Rees Howell Gronow, brief introductions to each part or segment of the book, and annotations (as footnotes and the very occasional translation in square brackets) to the text for the reader's convenience.

Readers should note: I have taken the liberty of modernising Gronow's punctuation, and even restructuring one or two of his anecdotes. On occasion, I have supplied the names of individuals – where known – suppressed in the original. These changes have been made with the modern reader in mind, with the simple aim of making Gronow's text as accessible as possible. Please also note that where Gronow gives sums of money in pounds sterling, these figures should be multiplied by a factor of 50, in order to give a rough modern equivalent.

To conclude, I can do no better than to quote from Gronow's own Preface to the first of his series of *Reminiscences,* published in 1861:

'In going over more than half a century, and treating of men and women and events, it was necessary to leave out many anecdotes which would, perhaps, have been more interesting than most of those that I have given;

for I would not willingly offend, or hurt the feelings of anyone, and I wish to respect the memory of the dead, as well as to take into consideration the sensitiveness of the living. My *Reminiscences*, it will be seen, are nothing more than miniature illustrations of contemporary history; and though the reader may find here and there scraps of biographical matter, I confine myself to facts and characteristics which were familiar to the circle in which I moved, and are perhaps as much public property as the painted portraits of the celebrities.'

Finally, I should like to thank the following individuals for tireless help and support: Paula Czaczkowska, Ewa Haren, Captain D. D. Horn (Curator of the Guards Museum, London), Evgenia and Jonathan North, John and Sylvia Summerville, and Anne Woodley.

Christopher Summerville
York, 2006

Rees Howell Gronow (1794-1865).

REES HOWELL GRONOW — A MINIATURE PORTRAIT

'Gronow was one of the prettiest dandy officers of proud Albion,' wrote M. H. de Villemessant in *Memoirs of a Journalist,* adding: 'He committed the greatest follies, without in the slightest disturbing the points of his shirt collar … and would rather have blown out his brains than have gone to the opera in morning costume …'

Rees Howell Gronow (1794–1865) was the eldest son of William Gronow, a wealthy Welsh landowner and deputy-lieutenant of the county of Glamorgan, and his wife, Anne, daughter of Rees Howell of Gwryd. He was educated at Eton College, where he counted P. B. Shelley, the poet, among his friends, and where the tyrannical headmaster, Dr John Keate ('a sort of pocket Hercules'), ruled by terror: 'I remember that the fear of the birch was so strong at the time that no boy went up to his lesson without trembling with apprehension of being put in the bill for a flogging.'

Having survived Keate's brutal regime, Gronow received an ensign's commission in the elite 1st Foot Guards on 24th December 1812. Somewhat small and slight in stature (his friends nicknamed him 'No-Grow'), the young officer's time was initially taken up in mounting guard at St James's Palace and learning how to powder his hair: 'I remember, when on guard, incurring the heavy displeasure of the late Duke of Cambridge for not having a sufficient quantity of powder on my head, and therefore presenting a somewhat piebald appearance. I received a strong reprimand from HRH, and he threatened even to place me under arrest should I ever appear again on guard in what he was pleased to call so slovenly and disgraceful a condition.'

Within a few short months, and having received little or no military training, Gronow was packed off to Spain, where he joined Wellington's army, and participated in the closing stages of the Peninsular War.

In the summer of 1814 Gronow was back in London, where he became a dandy and one of the few Guards officers admitted to Almack's assembly rooms, where, 'at those elegant balls' quadrilles and waltzes were the order of the day. And so, as a member of fashionable society, Gronow danced out the year, making new acquaintances, and observing that: 'It appears to be a law of natural history that every generation produces and throws out from the mob of society a few conspicuous men that pass under the general appellation of "men about town."' A suitable sobriquet, in fact, for Gronow himself, for soon he would become a noted dandy and deadly duellist, his portrait hanging in shop windows alongside those of the Prince Regent and 'Beau' Brummell.

A year later, the peace of Europe was shattered by Napoleon's escape from exile in Elba. With the emperor back on his throne, war was imminent, and by June 1815 Wellington and his redcoats were in Belgium and the countdown to battle had begun. Not wishing to miss the action, Gronow absented himself from his battalion in London, and funding his adventure with winnings at the gambling table, set off for Brussels as a member of General Picton's staff. Arriving in Belgium, Gronow attached himself to the Third Battalion of his regiment in time to become a participant in – and celebrated eyewitness of – the battle of Waterloo and its aftermath: 'When I call to mind how ill-rewarded our noble soldiers were for their heroic deeds, my heart bleeds for them. "Under the cold shade of aristocracy", men who in France would have been promoted for their valour to the highest grades of the army, lived and died, twenty or thirty years after the battle, with the rank of lieutenant or captain.' Gronow might well have included himself in this category: for though he was promoted Guards lieutenant ten days after Waterloo (with the equivalent Line rank of captain, which, needless to say, he adopted on retirement), he progressed no further, presumably lacking the £8,300 necessary to buy a majority. After spending some time with the Army of Occupation in Paris, Gronow finally quit the Army on 24th October 1821.

On 18th June 1823 – eight years to the day after the Great Battle – Gronow met his own personal Waterloo and was sentenced to gaol: having frittered away his fortune on fast living (like so many of his contemporaries), he was declared insolvent and imprisoned under the Insolvent Debtors Act. But with the death of his father in 1830 and his subsequent inheritance, Gronow was able to pay off his creditors, and the following year saw him established in Brummell's old house in Chesterfield Street, Mayfair, and once again energetically devoting himself to a life of idleness. This being the case, there was only one viable career option open to him: politics.

In 1832 Gronow was persuaded by Lord Yarborough to contest Grimsby for the Whigs, on condition that he promised not to employ bribery: 'I agreed to his conditions, and started the following morning for Lincolnshire … I immediately commenced my canvass, which continued for several days, and was apparently very successful. When the polling commenced, I thought myself sure of being elected, when, on the second day, an apparently respectable man, and one of my best supporters, came to me and said: "There are four persons of great influence to whom you must give £100 apiece. If you don't come in, I will engage to return the amount to you myself; and if you refuse to give the money, you are quite sure to be beaten."' Gronow refused and was beaten. His only consolation, perhaps, was that John Shelley, one of his Tory opponents, insisted on fawning over him on the hustings and treating him 'with such marked and studied politeness' as to make a complete fool of himself. The reason? Shelley – no doubt aware of his rival's reputation as a duellist – was convinced that Gronow would shoot him if beaten!

Weary of the political hothouse of Grimsby, Gronow next contested Stafford, and this time was determined to win: 'so I set to work to bribe every man, woman, and child in the ancient borough of Stafford. I engaged numerous agents, opened all the public houses that were not already taken by my opponents, gave suppers every night to my supporters, kissed all their wives and children, drank their health in every sort of abominable mixture, and secured my return against great local interest ... I sat during the whole of the first Reform Parliament for Stafford, but was beaten at the next general election by the long purse of Mr Holyoake, now Sir Francis Goodricke, Bart.'

'Abandoning hope of a further political career,' writes Christopher Hibbert in the *Oxford Dictionary of National Biography*, 'Gronow devoted the next thirty years to a life of idleness and fashionable pursuits in London and, later, in Paris, where he was present during the *coup d'état* of 1st – 2nd December 1851.'

It was in Paris that the journalist Villemessant encountered the captain: 'Mr Gronow, when I knew him, was small, spare, and about fifty years of age; his hair was thinning, and he wore a small moustache, of which the edge was daily shaved, which did not disguise the circumstance that the captain's latent vanity had recourse to brown dye. He always wore a blue tight-fitting coat, closely buttoned, just allowing a narrow line of white waistcoat to be visible ... the captain spent his days seated at the window, watching everyone he knew in Paris pass the "Petit Cercle", of which he was one of the founders, and where the latter part of his life was spent. This "Cercle" was a small and select club, occupying a suite of rooms in the Café de Paris, on the Boulevard des Italiens ... This little man, with his hair well arranged, scented, cold, and phlegmatic, knew the best people in Paris, visited all the diplomats, and was evidently intimate with everybody of note in Europe'

And it was in Paris that, according to Joseph Grego, 'After detailing his piquant store of anecdotes to his contemporaries for a couple of generations, Captain Gronow was induced to take up his pen.' In truth, motivated by the need to provide for himself and his family (although first married to Mademoiselle Didier of the Paris Opera, who bore him a daughter, Mathilde, Gronow later married a certain Mademoiselle de St Pol, who gave him a further four children), Gronow set to work to produce what John Raymond has called 'a public feat of reminiscence, written for cash with an immediate eye to the type of public that the writer knew so well.'

Gronow's first volume of 'fragmental and miniature illustrations of contemporary history' was a success, and a further three followed. The full set is as follows:

> *Reminiscences Of Captain Gronow, Formerly Of The Grenadier Guards And Member Of Parliament For Stafford, Being Anecdotes Of The Camp, The Court, And The Clubs, At The Close Of The Last War With France, Related By Himself,* London 1861.
>
> *Recollections And Anecdotes, Being A Second Series Of Reminiscences By Captain R. H. Gronow,* London 1863.
>
> *Celebrities Of London And Paris, Being A Third Series Of Reminiscences And Anecdotes,* London 1865.
>
> *Captain Gronow's Last Recollections, Being The Fourth And Final Series Of His Reminiscences And Anecdotes,* London 1866.

The last in the series, however, was published posthumously, for on 20th November 1865 Gronow died unexpectedly in Paris. His obituary in the *Gentlemen's Magazine* records: 'The *Morning Post* states that Captain Gronow has left a wife and four infant children wholly unprovided for, and that some friends in Paris are endeavouring to get up a subscription in their behalf ...'

PART

ONE

Two privates of the 1st Foot Guards in 1812. Gronow joined this regiment as an ensign in December of that year.

GENTLEMEN'S SONS

By the time the eighteen-year-old Gronow arrived in Spain, in October 1813, the war in the Iberian Peninsula was in its closing stages, having raged for almost six years. When Napoleon first lit the tinderbox, however, by launching his legions against a puny Portuguese Army in 1807, none – least of all he – could possibly have foretold the long struggle ahead, nor its momentous consequences.

At the end of 1807 Napoleon had defeated every army sent against him. Only Britain, protected by the English Channel and the wooden walls of its Royal Navy, stood between the emperor and European domination. Frustrated in his attempts to bring Perfidious Albion to the bargaining table, Napoleon decided to bring it to its knees by economic blockade. In essence, this meant waging a ruthless economic war on London by prohibiting British goods in Europe. In order for this so-called Continental System to work, however, the whole European coastline would have to be sealed off from British shipping. But Portugal, which enjoyed close trade links with London, refused to bend to the emperor's will, and the French invasion that followed effectively sparked off what became known as the Peninsular War.

When Napoleon's troops occupied Lisbon in December 1807 they did so with the connivance of Spain, a nominal ally of the French. This country was supposedly ruled by the elderly King Carlos IV, a weak and ineffective monarch, dominated by Luisa, his unfaithful and meddlesome queen, and undermined by Ferdinand, his treacherous and self-seeking son. But real power lay in the hands of Carlos's scheming Prime Minister, Manuel Godoy: an unpopular figure, who was reputed to be the queen's lover. Despite the formal alliance that bound Spain and France together, Godoy had been seeking a way of breaking ties with Napoleon ever since the destruction of the Spanish fleet – pressed into service alongside its French ally – at Trafalgar on 21st October 1805. Indeed, he had gone so far as to plot against Bonaparte with the emperor's Prussian enemies. Napoleon, fully aware of Godoy's treachery and Carlos's insecurity, decided that the day of reckoning was nigh, and used his expedition against Portugal as the pretext for stuffing Spain with troops. Thus, by a mixture of stealth and force, he determined to seize the whole Iberian Peninsula, bringing both defiant Portugal and faithless Spain under his direct control.

By May 1808, his forces had taken control of Madrid and a clutch of key Spanish cities, while Carlos and his dysfunctional family (supervised by Godoy) were stripped of their status and packed off to exile in France. Then, in short order, pro-French factions were 'persuaded' to elect Napoleon's elder brother, Joseph Bonaparte, king. The result of this breathtakingly cynical manoeuvre was a popular uprising – a 'war to the knife' – which blazed across the whole peninsula, and which conveniently opened the back door of Europe to British troops, who were promptly despatched to help the patriots evict the French.

The British campaign got off to a spectacular start, when, in a series of startling victories, Sir Arthur Wellesley kicked General Junot's French army out of Portugal in the summer of 1808. But the subsequent advance into Spain under Sir John Moore (Wellesley had been recalled to London), late in the year, was ill-timed and ill-coordinated, resulting in Moore's expeditionary force being chased at the sword's point to the port of Corunna and into the arms of the Royal Navy. By May 1809, however, Wellesley was back in Portugal, and having secured Lisbon as a base of operations, he proceeded to launch a methodical campaign aimed at ridding the whole peninsula of Napoleon's eagles.

By December 1812, the month that Gronow received his commission in the Guards, Wellesley (or the 1st Duke of Wellington as he was now known) had *achieved notable successes at Talavera, Busaco and Salamanca. A further crop of victories soon followed: in June 1813 he defeated Joseph Bonaparte at Vittoria; in July he was victorious at Sorauren; and in October, Wellington crossed the Bidassoa, taking the war into the south of France. Napoleon, having suffered severe reverses in Russia and Germany, was unable to stop this intrusion via the Pyrenees; nor, indeed, could he prevent the imminent full-scale invasion of France by Prussian, Russian and Austrian armies from the east.*

　　In November 1813 Wellington defeated Marshal Soult at the battle of the Nivelle. A month later, he was victorious again at the battle of the Nive. In January 1814 France was duly invaded by Britain's allies, and by 6 April, with Paris in Allied hands, Napoleon abdicated. News of this momentous event, however, did not reach the south of France before more blood was shed at the battle of Toulouse – another Wellingtonian victory – and at Bayonne, where the French launched a sortie against the British on the 14th. Three days later, however, Soult surrendered to Wellington, and the Peninsular War came to an end.

　　This long and bloody campaign – Napoleon's 'Spanish ulcer' – had played a major part in the emperor's fall. Taking the form of a double war – the first (a remarkably savage affair) against an enraged civilian population, the second (chivalrous in comparison) against Wellington's redcoats – the conflict had constituted a crippling drain on French manpower and materiel. Not least of all, by invading the Iberian Peninsula in 1807, Napoleon had inadvertently 'created' his nemesis: the Duke of Wellington. But what of Wellington's army, of which the young Gronow was now a member?

　　The fighting qualities of the duke's famous Peninsular army (the one with which he later claimed he could 'go anywhere and do anything') are legendary; but it is a curious fact that for the British Army of Gronow's day, military spectacle was placed above military efficiency. Musket barrels had to be 'as bright as a looking-glass' and all belts were pipe clayed pure white. Even leather knapsacks were varnished. Officers were instructed to comport themselves in a manner peculiar to their own regiment (overweight officers were advised to wear corsets), and the men obliged to wear stiff leather collars, designed to keep their heads erect at all times. Uniforms were gaudy and tight-fitting: scarlet for the infantry and heavy cavalry, dark blue for light cavalry and artillery, and dark green for riflemen. Officers' coatees were trimmed with gold or silver bullion and all headgear was designed to be tall and imposing, with ostrich plumes adding to the impression of height. Thus a soldier's sartorial performance was considered every bit as important as his combat performance.

Another peculiarity of the Wellingtonian military system was the degree to which the regiment, rather than the Army as a whole, constituted the soldier's spiritual, as well as corporeal, home. Indeed, as Myerly, points out, in British Military Spectacle, 'Rather than referring to "the Army" in the first half of the nineteenth century, it is more accurate to say that a collection of regiments was brought together temporarily to act in combination.' For the common soldiers, many of whom were refugees from poverty or the law (Wellington's so-called 'scum of the earth'), the regiment offered a kind of sanctuary and extended family. As for the officers, almost all of whom bought their commissions (unlike their French counterparts, who achieved their status through merit), the regiment constituted a socially exclusive club. And none was more elite than that to which Gronow belonged: the Foot Guards.

The three regiments of Foot Guards (which subsequently became the Grenadier Guards, the Coldstream Guards, and the Scots Guards, respectively – the Welsh Guards were not raised till 1915), were considered the cream of the Army. Guardsmen enjoyed higher pay and status than other soldiers, and officers' commissions had a purchase price approximately double that of the Line. As a result, the majority of Guards officers had aristocratic backgrounds – the so-called 'gentlemen's sons'. The quality of these officers varied greatly: some were competent and efficient; others lazy and foolish; some were true professionals; others rank amateurs, who had purchased commissions simply to escape boredom. In fact, the backbone of all regiments were the non-commissioned officers, who, in the Guards especially, were considered consummate professionals. Thus it was the corporals and sergeants who guided the young and inexperienced: both recruits and officers alike. As for the latter, Wellington complained that

they never read regulations or military manuals, and that 'every gentleman
proceeds according to his own fancy ...'

   A comment that held true in both war and peace. For once back home
at St James's, 'That area bounded by the Haymarket, along the south side
of Piccadilly to St James's Street, down to the Palace and along Pall Mall,
including the great park, thence to Charing Cross' (E. J. Burford, in Royal St
James's)*, the 'gentlemen's sons' – gilded with the laurels of victory and borne*
along by the euphoria prior to Napoleon's escape from Elba – continued to
proceed according to their reckless fancy, in the assembly rooms, clubs, coffee
houses, gambling hells, hotels, and theatres of the wealthiest quarter, of the
wealthiest city, of the wealthiest country in the world. Governed by the Prince
Regent from Carlton House, his mansion off Pall Mall – but led by George
Bryan 'Beau' Brummell, the 'king' of the Dandies – this was a place where,
according to Venetia Murray, in High Society: *'Gluttony and gambling were*
the fashionable vices ... and sexual morality, at least among a certain section
of the haut ton, virtually non-existent ...'

〜〜〜

🪶· Entrance Into The Army

After leaving Eton, I received an Ensign's commission[1] in the 1st Guards
during the month of December 1812. Though many years have elapsed,
I still remember my boyish delight at being named to so distinguished a
regiment, and at the prospect of soon taking a part in the glorious deeds
of our Army in Spain. I joined in February 1813 and cannot but recollect
with astonishment how limited and imperfect was the instruction which
an officer received at that time: he absolutely entered the Army without
any military education whatever. We were so defective in our drill, even
after we had passed out of the hands of the sergeant, that the excellence of
our non-commissioned officers alone prevented us from meeting with the
most fatal disasters in the face of enemy. Physical force and our bulldog

---

1 The lowest rank for an infantry officer.

energy carried many a hard-fought field. Luckily, *nous avons changé tout cela*[2] and our officers may now vie with those of any other Army in an age when the great improvements in musketry, in artillery practice, and in the greater rapidity of manoeuvring, have entirely changed the art of war, and rendered the individual education of those in every grade of command an absolute necessity.

After passing through the hands of the drill sergeant with my friends Dashwood, Batty, Browne, Lascelles, Hume and Master, and mounting guard at St James's for a few months, we were hurried off, one fine morning, in charge of a splendid detachment of 500 men to join Lord Wellington in Spain. Macadam had just begun to do for England what Marshal Wade did in Scotland seventy years before,[3] and we were able to march twenty miles a day with ease until we reached Portsmouth. There we found transports ready to convey a large reinforcement, of which we formed part, to Lord Wellington, who was now making his arrangements, after taking St Sebastian,[4] for a yet more important event in the history of the Peninsular War – the invasion of France.

🐝· Departure For And Arrival In Spain

We sailed under convoy of the *Madagascar* frigate, commanded by Captain Curtis, and after a favourable voyage, we arrived at Passages. Our stay there was short, for we were ordered to join the Army without loss of time. In three hours we got fairly into camp, where we were received with loud cheers by our brothers in arms.

The whole British Army was here under canvas, our allies, the Spaniards and Portuguese, being in the rear. About the middle of October, to our great delight, the Army received orders to cross the Bidassoa. At three o'clock on the morning of the 15th our regiment advanced through a

---

2 Literally 'we changed all that'.

3 John Loudon Macadam (1756–1836) was a road-builder who initiated the use of compacted stone: the word 'tarmac' is derived from his name.

4 This fortified Spanish port, which lay at the western end of the Pyrenees, fell to Sir Thomas Graham on 31st August 1813.

difficult country, and after a harassing march, reached the top of a hill as the grey light of morning began to dawn. We marched in profound silence but with a pleasurable feeling of excitement amongst all ranks at the thought of meeting the enemy, and perhaps with not an equally agreeable idea that we might be in the next world before the day was over.

As we ascended the rugged side of the hill, I saw for the first time, the immortal Wellington. He was accompanied by the Spanish General Alava, Lord Fitzroy Somerset, and Major, afterwards Colonel, Freemantle. He was very stern and grave-looking, he was in deep meditation, so long as I kept him in view, and spoke to no one. His features were bold and I saw much decision of character in his expression. He rode a knowing-looking, thoroughbred horse, and wore a grey overcoat, Hessian boots, and a large cocked hat.

We commenced the passage of the Bidassoa about five in the morning, and in a short time infantry, cavalry and artillery, found themselves upon French ground. The stream at the point we forded was nearly four feet deep, and had Soult been aware of what we were about, we should have found the passage of the river a very arduous undertaking.

Three miles above, we discovered the French Army and ere long found ourselves under fire. The sensation of being made a target to a large body of men is at first not particularly pleasant but, 'in a trice, the ear becomes more Irish, and less nice.' The first man I ever saw killed was a Spanish soldier, who was cut in two by a cannon ball. The French Army, not long after we began to return their fire, was in full retreat, and after a little sharp, but desultory fighting, in which our division met with some loss, we took possession of the camp and strong position of Soult's army. We found the soldiers' huts very comfortable: they were built of branches of trees and furze, and formed squares and streets, which had names placarded up, such as Rue de Paris, Rue de Versailles, etc. We were not sorry to find ourselves in such commodious quarters, as well as being well housed. The scenery surrounding the camp was picturesque and grand. From our elevated position, immediately in front, we commanded a wide and extensive plain, intersected by two important rivers, the Nive and the Nivelle. On the right, the lofty Pyrenees, with their grand and varied outline, stood forth conspicuously in a blue, cloudless sky. On our left was the Bay of Biscay, with our cruisers perpetually on the move.

We witnessed from the camp, one night about twelve o'clock, a fight at sea, between an English brig and a French corvette, which was leaving the Adour with provisions and ammunition. She was chased by the brig and brought to action. The night was sufficiently clear to enable us to discover distinctly the position of the vessels and the measured flash of their guns. They were at close quarters and in less than half an hour we discovered the crew of the corvette taking to their boats. Shortly afterwards the vessel blew up with a loud explosion. We came to the conclusion that sea-fighting was more agreeable than land-fighting, as the crews of the vessels engaged without previous heavy marching, and with loose light clothing, there was no manoeuvring or standing for hours on the defensive, the wounded were immediately taken below and attended to, and the whole affair was over in a pleasingly brief period.

☞· Camp Life During The Peninsular War

There was a wide difference in the camp life of the English and French armies. An English soldier in camp appeared to be the most uncomfortable of mortals, there was no plan laid down for his recreation, or the employment of his leisure hours, and you might see him either brushing his clothes or cleaning his accoutrements, or else sitting on his knapsack, smoking his pipe to pass the time. We had no large tent wherein the men could congregate to converse, read, or otherwise amuse themselves, and when the weather was wet, they huddled together in small tents, where the atmosphere was worse than that of the Black Hole of Calcutta. The pipe clay system of tormenting our men, by requiring them to keep their kits clean, and punishing them by extra drills if the firelock or belts were not as spotless as on parade at the Horse Guards, was (to say the least of it) extremely injudicious.

The French soldiers, on the other hand, had small tents, amply large enough for five or six men, or in default of these, they constructed tents with earth, trees, and rushes. Streets were formed, with squares; places of amusement were planned, and large trenches were dug in every direction, to drain the ground thoroughly. The officers, if near a town, took possession of the best lodgings, for the convenience of coffee-houses and kitchens, but although they had every luxury they could afford or procure, their motto was, *À la guerre comme la guerre*. On entering a French camp you saw as much order as in the best regulated towns. Gendarmes kept strict watch over the soldiers, a fire brigade was always in readiness, and everything was arranged methodically. The dress of the French soldier was not only loose and comfortable, but easily cleaned, and his knapsack was remarkable for its convenience. A *cantinière*[5] was attached to the camp, and supplied the officers and men with wine and spirits according to regulations.

The French soldier marched quicker than the English, both in advance and retreat, and after a victory by our troops few prisoners were taken. The Duke of Wellington, with all his wonderful foresight and genius, could never get at the secret why so few stragglers were met with in following the enemy, whereas at Burgos, after our raising the siege of that town, indescribable confusion arose, and nearly half the English Army were either left behind or taken prisoners by Soult and Clauzel.[6]

The system of outposts in the French Army was on a different footing from ours. Before the enemy, the French sentinel was relieved every hour, whereas our soldiers remained on duty two hours! The extra hour caused great fatigue and in cold weather induced sleep. A troop of the 11th Light Dragoons on duty in front – that is, at the extreme vedette – in the immediate presence of the enemy was once caught napping. The French officer in command, observing the bad guard kept, ordered forward a sergeant and five men, who entered our lines and found Captain Wood and his men fast asleep. When the dragoons awoke, they were compelled to surrender themselves prisoners of war. Now, if the vedette had been

---

5 A sutleress, quite often a soldier's wife, selling food and drink.

6 According to Napier, in *History of the War in the Peninsula*, 'The whole loss of the … retreat cannot … be set down at less than 9,000, including the loss in the siege.' This from a total of some 32,000 Anglo-Portuguese soldiers.

changed every hour, this disgraceful catastrophe would not have occurred. Doubtless all these matters are better arranged now: the Crimean War [7] ought to have taught us many valuable lessons, and our experience, so dearly bought, should be made profitable for the future. Were we to take a leaf out of the French book of tactics, instead of following the German school in all its pedantries, our armies would be better prepared for active service than they now are.

🐟· Uniform And Bearing Of The French Soldier

The French infantry soldier averaged five feet, five or six inches in height. In build they were much about what they are now, perhaps a little broader over the shoulder. They were smart, active, handy fellows, and much more able to look after their personal comforts than British soldiers, as their camps indicated. The uniform of those days consisted of a shako, which spread out at the top, a short-waisted, swallow-tailed coat, and large, baggy trousers and gaiters. The clothing of the French soldier was roomy and enabled him to move about at ease (no pipe clay accessories occupied their attention). In a word, their arms and accoutrements were infinitely superior to our own, taking into consideration the practical necessities of warfare. Their muskets were inferior to ours and their firing less deadly. The cavalry we thought badly horsed but their uniforms, though showy, were like those of the infantry, comfortably large and roomy.

I have frequently remarked that firearms are of little use to the mounted soldier, and often an encumbrance to man and horse. Cavalry want only arm: the sabre. Let the men be well mounted, and at home in the saddle. It requires great knowledge in a commander-in-chief to know when and how to use his cavalry. It has been my misfortune to witness oft-repeated blunders in the employment of the best-mounted regiments in the world. I consider the French generals had more knowledge of the use of cavalry than our own, when a great battle was to be fought.

---

7 Fought against Russia, 1853–56.

🎣· Dysentery In The Peninsula

Early in the year 1812 the Duke of York despatched to the seat of war the 3rd Battalion of my old regiment. It was considered by military men to have been the finest in His Majesty's service. All the men, with the exception of the grenadier company, were strong, active young fellows, but had not seen active service. They were conveyed to Cadiz, in men-of-war, and arrived there without any accident, but owing to change of diet, and the substituting the horrid wine of the country for the porter they had been accustomed to at home, before the expiration of a few weeks, 500 of these fine fellows died in the hospital at Vizu, and were buried in the churchyard there. I mention this to show how careful commanding officers ought to be to prevent similar consequences from decimating bodies of fresh troops, although warnings of this sort have occurred all over the globe.

On joining my regiment in the peninsula, one of the grenadiers, a tall and well-built man, was recommended to me as the best person to employ for pitching my tent. This man had been brought up as a carpenter but through some misunderstanding with his relations had enlisted. While cutting the trench he entered into conversation with me, and said he hoped, as I appeared very young and unaccustomed to bivouacking, that I would forgive him for being so bold as to offer a little salutary advice: which was, to drink every morning on rising, a small glass of brandy or rum, as by so doing rheumatism, dysentery, and many other camp disorders, would be prevented. He added, with tears in his eyes, that he had lost his brother at Vizu, owing to his not following the advice he was now giving me. I was so struck with the earnest manner of the man that I adopted his panacea, and during the whole time that I was in camp I never had a day's illness.

🎣· My Soldier-Servant

When in Spain with my regiment, it fell to my lot to receive from the ranks a soldier born in Sicily, of Sicilian parentage, by name Proyd. When the Guards occupied Catania, this individual, having lost his father and mother, was adopted by the regiment, and through the instrumentality of Lord Proby, became a soldier, and was inscribed on the muster-roll of the 1st Foot Guards. He was an excellent servant, and perhaps the best caterer in the Army, for when we were invading the Pyrenees, he supplied me with every delicacy, while the Army generally was living on salt beef and biscuits: in fact, poultry, mutton, and fresh bread at my table were the rule, rather than the exception. With all these accomplishments, he possessed one fault: a too great admiration, unqualified with respect, for the charms of the fair sex, and he seldom lost an opportunity of stealing a kiss from any pretty girl that came in his way.

On our return from the peninsula, I took this Figaro[8] with me to White Knights, the seat of the Duke of Marlborough, where I was invited to spend some days. At this charming house I found a great number of visitors, among whom were Lord and Lady Grenville, Lord and Lady Macclesfield, Mr Mathias, the author of *The Pursuits of Literature,* Lord William Fitzroy, Mr Garlick, and others. It happened on the day of my arrival that my servant met the maid of Lady Macclesfield on the staircase, and without the slightest ceremony he attempted to kiss her. The maid, unaccustomed to such behaviour, screamed, ran downstairs, and then up again, with Proyd close at her heels – he even followed her into her lady's room, where she flew to take refuge. Her ladyship, alarmed at seeing a strange man in her room, shrieked loudly, many persons ran to her assistance, and her noble husband, more dead than alive, thinking some sad disaster had befallen the countess, inquired with caution, 'What is the matter?' Her ladyship replied in a faint voice, 'The man is under the bed.' Pokers and tongs were seized, and the noble lord made use of his weapons to such purpose that the delinquent quietly surrendered. This incident, which created great confusion, rendered it necessary that the Sicilian should be sent to rejoin his regiment. Poor Proyd soon after applied for his discharge, and returned to his native land to make love to his own countrywomen.

---

8   A reference to the comic valet in Beaumarchais' play made famous by Mozart's 1786 opera, 'Le Nozze di Figaro'.

⇒· Major General Stewart And Lord Wellington

If the present generation of Englishmen would take the trouble of looking at the newspaper, which fifty years ago informed the British public of passing events both at home and abroad, they would, doubtless, marvel at the very limited and imperfect amount of intelligence which the best journals were enabled to place before their readers (the progress of the Peninsular campaign was very imperfectly chronicled). It will, therefore, be easily imagined what interest was attached to certain letters that appeared in the *Morning Chronicle,* which criticised with much severity and frequently with considerable injustice, the military movements of Lord Wellington's Spanish campaigns.

The attention of the commander-in-chief being drawn to these periodical and personal comments on his conduct of the war, his lordship at once perceived, from the information which they contained, that they must have been written by an officer holding a high command under him. Determined to ascertain the author – who, in addressing a public journal, was violating the Articles of War and, it might be, assisting the enemy – means were employed in London to identify the writer. The result was that Lord Wellington discovered the author of the letters to be no other than Sir Charles Stewart, the late Lord Londonderry. As soon as Lord Wellington had made himself master of this fact, he summoned Sir Charles Stewart to headquarters at Torres Vedras and on his appearance, he, without the least preface, addressed him thus: 'Charles Stewart, I have ascertained with deep regret that you are the author of the letters which appeared in the *Morning Chronicle,* abusing me and finding fault with my military plans.'

Lord Wellington here paused for a moment and then continued: 'Now, Stewart, you know your brother Castlereagh is my best friend, to whom I owe everything, nevertheless, if you continue to write letters to the *Chronicle,* or any other newspaper, by God, I will send you home.'

Sir Charles Stewart was so affected at this rebuke that he shed tears and expressed himself deeply penitent for the breach of confidence and want of respect for the Articles of War. They immediately shook hands and parted friends. It happened, however, that Sir Charles Stewart did not remain long in the cavalry, of which he was adjutant-general. Within a few weeks he was named one of the commissioners deputed to proceed to the Allied Armies, where the sovereigns were then completing their plans to crush Napoleon.[9]

Sir John Waters

Amongst the distinguished men in the Peninsular War whom my memory brings occasionally before me, is the well-known and highly popular Quartermaster-General Sir John Waters, who was born at Margam, a Welsh village in Glamorganshire. He was one of those extraordinary persons that seem created by kind Nature for particular purposes, and without using the word in an offensive sense, he was the most admirable spy that was ever attached to the Army. One would almost have thought that the Spanish War was entered upon in order to display his remarkable qualities. He could assume the character of Spaniards of every degree and station, so as to deceive the most acute of those whom he delighted to imitate. In the *posada* [tavern] of the village he was hailed by the contrabandist or the muleteer as one of their own race; in the lively assemblies he was an accomplished *hidalgo* [squire]; at the bullfight the toreador received his congratulations as from one who had encountered the *toro* in the arena; in the church he would converse with the friar upon the number of Ave Marias and Paternostas which could lay a ghost, or tell him the history of everyone who had perished by the flame of the Inquisition, relating his crime – whether carnal or anti-Catholic – and he could join in the *seguadilla* or in the *guaracha* [popular dances].

But what rendered him more efficient than all was his wonderful power of observation and accurate description, which made the information he gave so reliable and valuable to the Duke of Wellington. Nothing escaped him. When amidst a group of persons, he would minutely watch the

---

9 In fact, Stewart was sent as British representative to the Allied Headquarters by his elder brother, foreign secretary Castlereagh: there, according to Haythornthwaite, in *Who's Who in the Napoleonic Wars*, Stewart 'was never afraid to speak his mind, even to the commanders-in-chief, and gained a reputation for eccentric behaviour.'

movement, attitude, and expression of every individual that composed it; in the scenery by which he was surrounded he would carefully mark every object (not a tree, not a bush, not a large stone, escaped his observation); and it was said that in a cottage he noted every piece of crockery on the shelf, every domestic utensil, and even the number of knives and forks that were got ready for use at dinner.

His acquaintance with the Spanish language was marvellous: from the finest works of Calderon to the ballads in the *patois* of every province, he could quote, to the infinite delight of those with whom he associated. He could assume any character that he pleased: he could be the Castilian, haughty and reserved; the Asturian, stupid and plodding; the Catalonian, intriguing and cunning; the Andalusian, laughing and merry. In short, he was all things to all men. Nor was he incapable of passing off, when occasion required, for a Frenchman (but as he spoke the language with a strong German accent, he called himself an Alsatian). He maintained that character with the utmost nicety, and as there is a strong feeling of fellowship – almost equal to that which exists in Scotland – amongst all those who are born in the departments of France bordering the Rhine and who maintain their Teutonic originality, he always found friends and supporters in every regiment of the French service.

He was on one occasion entrusted with a very difficult mission by the Duke of Wellington, which he undertook effectually to perform, and to return on a particular day with the information that was required.

Great was the disappointment when it was ascertained beyond a doubt that just after leaving the camp he had been taken prisoner before he had time to exchange his uniform. Such, however, was the case: a troop of dragoons had intercepted him and carried him off, and the commanding officer desired two soldiers to keep a strict watch over him and carry him to headquarters. He was of course disarmed and being placed on a horse, was, after a short time, galloped off by his guards. He slept one night under durance vile [i.e. imprisonment] at a small inn, where he was allowed to remain in the kitchen. Conversation flowed on very glibly, and as he appeared a stupid Englishman, who could not understand a word of

French or Spanish, he was allowed to listen, and thus obtained precisely the intelligence that he was in search of. The following morning, being again mounted, he overheard a conversation between his guards, who deliberately agreed to rob and shoot him at a mill where they were to stop, and to report to their officer that they had been compelled to fire at him in consequence of his attempt to escape.

Shortly before they arrived at the mill, for fear that they might meet with someone who would insist on having a portion of the spoil, the dragoons took from their prisoner his watch and his purse, which he surrendered with good grace. On their arrival at the mill they dismounted, and in order to give some appearance of truth to their story, they went into the house, leaving their prisoner outside, in the hope that he would make some attempt to escape. In an instant, Waters threw his cloak upon a neighbouring olive bush and mounted his cocked hat on the top. Some empty flour sacks lay upon the ground, and a horse laden with well-filled flour sacks stood at the door. Sir John contrived to enter one of the empty sacks and throw himself across the horse. When the soldiers came out of the house they fired their carbines at the supposed prisoner and galloped off at the utmost speed.

A short time after, the miller came out and mounted his steed. The general contrived to rid himself of the encumbrance of the sack, and sat up, riding behind the man, who, suddenly turning round saw a ghost – as he believed – for the flour that still remained in the sack had completely whitened his fellow-traveller and given him a most unearthly appearance. The frightened miller was 'putrefied' – as Mrs Malaprop would say – at the sight, and a push from the white spectre brought the unfortunate man to the ground, when away rode the gallant quartermaster with his sacks of flour, which, at length bursting, made a ludicrous spectacle of man and horse.

On reaching the English camp, where Lord Wellington was anxiously deploring his fate, a sudden shout from the soldiers made his Lordship turn round, when a figure, resembling the statue in 'Don Juan'[10] galloped

10 A reference to the talking graveyard statue of *Il Commendatore*, in Mozart's 1787 opera, 'Don Giovanni'.

up to him. The duke, affectionately shaking him by the hand said, 'Waters, you never deceived me yet, and though you come in a most questionable shape, I must congratulate you and myself.'

When this story was told at the clubs, one of those listeners who always want something more, called out, 'Well, and what did Waters say?' To which Alvanley replied, 'Oh, Waters made a very *flowery* speech, like a well-bred man.'

🦫· St Jean De Luz

During the winter of 1813 the Guards were stationed with headquarters at St Jean de Luz, and most comfortable we managed to make them. For some short time previously we had been on scanty commons, and had undergone considerable privation: indeed we might have said, like the colonel to Johnny Newcome on his arrival to join his regiment, 'We sons of Mars have long been fed on brandy and cigars.'[11]

I had no cause to complain personally, for my servant, a Sicilian, was one of the most accomplished foragers (ill-natured persons might give him a worse name) in the whole Army, and when others were nearly starving, he always managed to provide meat or poultry. He rode on his mule sometimes from twenty to thirty miles, often running the greatest dangers, to procure me a good meal, of which he took care to have, very justly, a large share for himself.

At St Jean de Luz, we were more attentive to our devotions than we had been for some time. Divine service was performed punctually every Sunday on the sand hills near the town. Lord Wellington and his numerous staff placed themselves in the midst of our square, and his lordship's chaplain read the service, to which Lord Wellington always appeared to listen with great attention.

The mayor of the town, thinking to please 'the great English lord', gave a ball at the Hôtel de Ville: our commander-in-chief did not go, but was represented by Waters. I was there, and expected to see some of the young

---

11 From Thomas Rowland's satirical cartoon, *The Military Adventures of Johnny Newcombe.*

ladies of the country, so famed for their beauty: they were, however, far too patriotic to appear, and the only lady present was Lady Waldegrave, then living with her husband at headquarters. What was one partner among so many? The ball was a dead failure, in spite of the efforts of the mayor, who danced – to our intense amusement – an English hornpipe, which he had learnt in not a very agreeable manner, viz., when a prisoner of war in the hulks at Plymouth.

There were two packs of hounds at St Jean de Luz: one kept by Lord Wellington, the other by Marsden, of the Commissariat. Our officers went uncommonly straight. Perhaps our best man across country (though sometimes somewhat against his will) was the late Colonel Lascelles of my regiment, like myself, a mere lad. He rode a horse seventeen hands high, called Bucephalus, which invariably ran away with him, and more than once nearly capsized Lord Wellington. The good living at St Jean de Luz agreed so well with my friend that he waxed fat, and from that period to his death was known to the world by the jovial appellation of Bacchus Lascelles.

Shortly before we left St Jean de Luz, we took our turn of outposts in the neighbourhood of Bidart, a large village, about ten miles from Bayonne. Early one frosty morning in December, an order came, that if we saw the enemy advancing, we were not to fire or give the alarm. About five, we perceived two battalions wearing grenadier caps coming on. They turned out to belong to a Nassau regiment,[12] which had occupied the advanced post of the enemy, and hearing that Napoleon had met with great reverses in Germany, signified to us their intention to desert. They were a fine-looking body of men and appeared, I thought, rather ashamed of the step they had taken. On the same day we were relieved and on our way back met Lord Wellington with his hounds. He was dressed in a light-blue frock-coat (the colour of the Hatfield hunt) which had been sent out to him as a present from Lady Salisbury, then one of the leaders of the fashionable world and an enthusiastic admirer of his lordship.

---

12 Troops from the Duchy of Nassau, one of Napoleon's clutch of German satellites, and a member of his Confederation of the Rhine.

Here, I remember seeing for the first time, a very remarkable character, the Honourable W. Dawson, of my regiment. He was surrounded by muleteers, with whom he was bargaining to provide carriage for innumerable hampers of wine, liqueurs, hams, potted meat, and other good things which he had brought from England. He was a particularly gentlemanly and amiable man, much beloved by the regiment. No one was so hospitable or lived so magnificently. His cooks were the best in the Army and he had a host of servants of all nations – Spaniards, French, Portuguese, Italians – who were employed in scouring the country for provisions. Lord Wellington once honoured him with his company, and on entering the ensign's tent, found him alone at table, with a dinner fit for a king, his plate and linen in good keeping, and his wines perfect. Lord Wellington was accompanied on this occasion by Sir Edward Pakenham and Colonel du Burgh, afterwards Lord Downes.

It fell to my lot to partake of his princely hospitality and dine with him at his quarters, a farmhouse in a village on the Bidassoa, and I never saw a better dinner put upon table. The career of this amiable Amphitryon,[13] to our great regret, was cut short, after exercising for about a year, a splendid but not very wise hospitality. He had only a younger brother's fortune, his debts became very considerable, and he was obliged to quit the Guards. He and his friends had literally eaten up his little fortune.

⇗• Foolhardiness
I may here recount an instance of the folly and foolhardiness of youth, and the recklessness to which a long course of exposure to danger produces. When Bayonne was invested,[14] I was one night on duty on the outer picket. The ground inside the breastwork, which had been thrown up for our protection by Burgoyne, was in a most disagreeable state for anyone who wished to repose after the fatigues of the day, being knee-deep in mud of a remarkably plastic nature. I was dead tired and determined to get a little rest in some more agreeable spot, so calling my sergeant, I told

13 A mythological Greek prince, whose name has come to mean a good or generous host.
14 The siege of this southern French city ran from 23rd February – 27th April 1814.

him to give me his knapsack for a pillow: I would make a comfortable night of it on the top of the breastwork, as it was an invitingly dry place. 'For heaven's take care, sir,' said he, 'you'll have fifty bullets in you. You will be killed to a certainty.' 'Pooh, nonsense,' said I, and climbing up, I wrapt myself in my cloak, laid my head on the knapsack, and soon fell into a sound sleep.

By the mercy of Providence I remained in a whole skin, either from the French immediately underneath not perceiving me or not thinking me worth a shot. But when General Stopford came up with Lord James Hay (who not long since reminded me of this youthful escapade), I received a severe wigging and was told to consider myself lucky that I was not put under arrest for exposing my life in so foolish a manner.

⟿· Discipline

When the headquarters of the Army were at St Jean de Luz, Soult made a movement in front of our right centre, which the English general took for a reconnaissance. As the French general perceived that we had ordered preparations to receive him, he sent a flag of truce to demand a cessation of hostilities, saying that he wanted to shoot an officer and several men for acts of robbery committed by them, with every sort of atrocity, on the farmers and peasantry of the country. The execution took place in view of both armies, and a terrible lesson it was. I cannot specify the date of this event, but think it must have been the latter end of November 1813. About the same time General Harispe, who commanded a corps of Basques, issued a proclamation forbidding the peasantry to supply the English with provisions or forage, on pain of death. It stated that we were savages, and, as a proof of this, our horses were born with short tails! I saw this absurd proclamation, which was published in French and in the Basque languages, and distributed all over the country.

Before we left the neighbourhood of Bayonne for Bordeaux, a soldier was hanged for robbery, on the sands of the Adour. This sort of punishment astonished the French almost as much as it did the soldier. On a march we were very severe, and if any of our men were caught committing an act of violence or brigandage, the offender was tried by a drumhead court martial and hanged in a very short time.

Among the numerous bad characters in our ranks, several were coiners, or utterers of bad money. In the second brigade of Guards, just before we arrived at St Jean de Luz, a soldier was convicted of this offence and was sentenced to receive 800 lashes. This man made sham Spanish dollars out of the pewter spoons of the regiment. As he had before been convicted and flogged, he received this terrible sentence and died under the lash. Would it not have been better to have condemned him to be shot? It would have been more humane, certainly more military, and far less brutal.[15]

I knew an officer of the 18th Hussars, 'W. R.', young, rich, and a fine-looking fellow, who joined the Army not far from St Sebastian. His stud of horses was remarkable for their blood, his grooms were English, and three in number. He brought with him a light cart to carry forage, and a *fourgon* [wagon] for his own baggage. All went well till he came to go on outpost duty, but not finding there any of the comforts to which he had been accustomed, he quietly mounted his charger, told his astonished sergeant that campaigning was not intended for a gentleman, and instantly galloped off to his quarters, ordering his servants to pack up everything immediately, as he had hired a transport to take him off to England. He left us before anyone had time to stop him, and though despatches were sent off to the commander-in-chief, requesting that a court martial might sit to try the young deserter, he arrived home long enough before the despatches to enable him to sell out of his regiment. He deserved to have been shot.

✿• The Battle Of The Nive
We expected to remain quietly in our winter quarters at St Jean de Luz, but to our surprise, early one morning, we were aroused from sleep by the

---

15 According to Sir Charles Oman, in *Wellington's Army*, 'For the rank and file flogging was the universal panacea' with the number of strokes ranging from a minimum of twenty-five for petty crimes, up to a lethal 1,200 for such serious offences as desertion or striking an officer.'

beating of the drum calling us to arms. We were soon in marching order. It appeared that our outposts had been severely pushed by the French, and we were called upon to support our companions in arms.

The whole of the British Army, as well as the division of the Guards, had commenced a forward movement. Soult, seeing this, entirely changed his tactics, and from that time – viz., 9th December – a series of engagements took place. The fighting on the 9th was comparatively insignificant. When we were attacked on the 10th, the Guards held the mayor's house and the grounds and orchards attached. This was an important station.

Large bodies of the enemy's infantry approached, and after desultory fighting, succeeded in penetrating our position, when many hand-to-hand combats ensued. Towards the afternoon, officers and men having displayed great gallantry, we drove the enemy from the ground which they courageously disputed with us, and from which they eventually retreated to Bayonne. Every day there was constant fighting along the whole of our line, which extended from the sea to the Lower Pyrenees: a distance probably not less than thirty miles.

On the 11th we only exchanged a few shots, but on the 12th Soult brought into action from fifteen to twenty thousand men, and attacked our left with a view of breaking our line. One of the most remarkable incidents of the 12th was the fact of an English battalion being surrounded by a division of French in the neighbourhood of the mayor's house, which, as before observed, was one of our principal strategical positions. The French commanding officer, believing that no attempt would be made to resist, galloped up to the officer of the British regiment and demanded his sword. Upon this, without the least hesitation, the British officer shouted out, 'This fellow wants us to surrender: charge, my boys! and show them what stuff we are made of.' Instantaneously a hearty cheer rang out, and our men rushed forward impetuously, drove off the enemy at the point of the bayonet, and soon disposed of the surrounding masses. In a few minutes, they had taken prisoners, or killed, the whole of the infantry regiment opposed to them.

On the 13th was fought the bloody battle of the Nivelle.[16] Soult had determined to make a gigantic effort to drive us back into Spain. During the night of the 12th, he rapidly concentrated about 60,000 troops in front of Sir Rowland Hill's *corps d'armée,* consisting of 15,000 men,[17] who occupied a very strong position, which was defended by some of the best artillery in the world. At daybreak, Sir Rowland Hill was astonished to find himself threatened by masses of infantry advancing over a country luckily intersected by rivulets, hedges, and woods, which prevented the enemy from making a rapid advance, whilst, at the same time, it was impossible on such ground to employ cavalry. Sir Rowland, availing himself of an elevated position, hurriedly surveyed his ground, and concentrated his men at such points as he knew the nature of the field would induce the enemy to attack. The French, confident of success from their superior numbers, came gallantly up, using the bayonet for the first time in a premeditated attack. Our men stood their ground and for hours acted purely on the defensive, being sustained by the admirable practice of our artillery, whose movements no difficulty of ground could, on this occasion, impede, so efficiently were the guns horsed, and so perfect was the training of the officers. It was not until midday that the enemy became discouraged at finding that they were unable to make any serious impression on our position: they then retired in good order, Sir Rowland Hill not daring to follow them.

Lord Wellington arrived just in time to witness the end of the battle and while going over the field with Sir Rowland Hill, he remarked that he had never seen so many men *hors de combat* in so small a space.

I must not omit to mention a circumstance which occurred during this great fight, alike illustrative of cowardice and of courage. The colonel of an infantry regiment, who shall be nameless, being hard pressed, showed a disposition not only to run away himself, but to order his regiment to retire. In fact, a retrograde movement had commenced, when my gallant and

---

16 The Nivelle was fought on 10th November 1813 – the action fought on 13th December was the Combat of St-Pierre-d'Irube, a postscript to the battle of the Nive.

17 According to David Chandler, in his *Dictionary of the Napoleonic Wars,* Soult's force numbered 42,000 and Hill's 14,000.

dear friend Lord Charles Churchill, aide-de-camp to Sir William Stewart, dashed forward, and, seizing the colours of the regiment, exclaimed, 'If your colonel will not lead you, follow me, my boys!' The gallantry of this youth, then only eighteen years of age, so animated the regiment, and restored their confidence, that they rallied and shared in the glory of the day.

🐊· The Light Company's Poodle And Sir F. Ponsonby

Every regiment has a pet of some sort or another. One distinguished Highland regiment possesses a deer, the Welsh Fusiliers a goat, which is the object of their peculiar affection, and which generally marches with the band. The light company of my battalion of the lst Guards, in 1813, rejoiced in a very handsome poodle, which had, if I mistake not, been made prisoner at Vittoria. At the commencement of the battle of 9th December 1813, near the mayor's house, not far from Bidart, we observed the gallant Frederick Ponsonby[18] well in front with the skirmishers, and by the side of his horse the soldiers' poodle. The colonel was encouraging our men to advance and the poodle, in great glee, was jumping and barking at the bullets, as they flew round him like hail. On a sudden, we observed Ponsonby struggling with a French mounted officer, whom he had already disarmed, and was endeavouring to lead off to our lines, when the French skirmishers, whose numbers had increased, fired several shots and wounded Ponsonby, forcing him to relinquish his prisoner and retire. At the same time, a bullet broke one of the poor dog's legs. For his gallant conduct in this affair, the poodle became, if possible, a still greater favourite than he was before and his friends, the men of the light company, took him to England, where I saw my three-legged friend for several years afterwards, the most prosperous of poodles, and the happiest of the canine race.

🐊· The Guards And The Umbrellas

During the action of 10th December 1813, commonly known as that of the Mayor's House, in the neighbourhood of Bayonne, the Grenadier Guards,

---

18 Sir Frederick Cavendish Ponsonby (1783–1837), colonel of the 12th Light Dragoons.

under the command of Colonel Tynling, occupied an unfinished redoubt on the right of the high road. The Duke of Wellington happened to pass with Freemantle and Lord A. Hill, on his return to headquarters, having satisfied himself that the fighting was merely a feint on the part of Soult. His Grace on looking around saw, to his surprise, a great many umbrellas, with which the officers protected themselves from the rain that was then falling. Arthur Hill came galloping up to us saying, 'Lord Wellington does not approve of the use of umbrellas during enemy's firing, and will not allow "the gentlemen's sons" to make themselves ridiculous in the eyes of the Army.' Colonel Tynling, a few days afterwards, received a wigging from Lord Wellington for suffering his officers to carry umbrellas in the face of the enemy, his Lordship observing: 'The Guards may in uniform, when on duty at St James's, carry them if they please, but in the field it is not only ridiculous but unmilitary.'

⤙· A Foraging Party On The Adour

Early in the spring of 1814 I was ordered to proceed with Lord James Hay on a foraging expedition. Our party consisted of fifty men, armed with firelocks, and mounted upon mules. It would be impossible to give any adequate idea of our zigzag march and our wanderings in the dark. At last, after proceeding in tolerably good order for about nine hours, we came in sight of a village called Dax, consisting of a few pretty houses, about a mile distant.

At break of day, wanting our accustomed breakfast, we determined to seek quarters there, but gave directions to the non-commissioned officers to prevent the slightest disorder or pillage. My batman, Proyd, who spoke nearly every European language, advanced into the market place with a saucepan, which he had brought with him from camp, and began striking it with a thick stick with all his might. The noise awoke the inhabitants, some of whom approached our party, and after much persuasion, one of them was prevailed upon by Lord James to show us the mayor's house, and presently this personage, 'dressed in a little brief authority,' made his appearance. We told him that one object of our coming was to procure provisions for ourselves, and forage for our horses and mules, but that everything supplied should be paid for. The mayor regarded us with suspicion, until Proyd entered with our teacups and boiling water, and asked in good French for some plates for 'My lord.' The title of 'My lord' electrified the mayor, and in less than a quarter of an hour the whole of his family appeared, and offered us and our men everything that we required.

With a heart full of thankfulness I sat down to an excellent breakfast of cold meat, eggs, coffee, and bread and butter, and, to crown all, one of the daughters of the mayor, an extremely elegant young lady, entered the room with some delicious comfitures, of which she said her mother begged our acceptance. The wife of the mayor soon after joined us, and to our astonishment and delight, began conversing with us in English. She said that she had been brought up in England, and that her mother was English, but had left her native land for France when she was about sixteen.

Having refreshed ourselves, and seen that the horses and mules had been properly groomed and baited, we gave orders to return, and our troop put itself again in motion, the animals being laden with straw, Indian corn, and forage of every description, for which we paid the mayor in Spanish dollars. After we had marched some hours, finding that, hampered as we were, we could not march well in the dark, we determined to halt at the first village we fell in with, and continue our march the next morning to Bayonne, whence we were then about eight leagues distant.[19] We soon struck a little bourg about two leagues from Dax, but could see no one stirring in the place: in fact, it seemed deserted. However, Proyd, ever alert, heard a dog bark in one of the houses, a sign that the inhabitants were hiding. We knocked first at one house and then at another, until our patience began to be exhausted, when a sleepy-looking fellow popped his head out of a window and asked us in a most insolent manner what we wanted. While we were parleying with him, one of the sergeants, an active young fellow, scrambled up to the window from whence this Caliban was jeering at us,

19 Presumably these are English leagues, one of which equals three miles.

bolted down the stairs, opened the front door, and admitted us into the house. It turned out to be the cabaret of the village, and it was the landlord who had just greeted us in this abusive manner. He was evidently an inveterate enemy of the British, for he would neither give us any information as to how our men were to be billeted, nor show us even common civility. However, finding our host so contumacious, we ordered him to be placed in durance vile, determining to carry him off to headquarters as a prisoner.

The next morning a council of war was held to devise a plan for transporting our prisoner. Proyd, the Figaro of the party, suggested placing him upon a mule, but the question was, how to get him mounted on the back of one at so early an hour in the morning, without creating a disturbance in the village. Hay, however, had no scruples on that score, and gave instructions to have the prisoner tied upon one of the animals. Proyd, approaching the fellow from behind, threw one of the regimental bags over his head, and with the aid of his comrades fastened him securely on a mule. When all was arranged to our satisfaction, the man began to bellow, and his neighbour, finding we were in earnest, came out and begged for mercy, but to no purpose, for we were determined to make an example of the disobliging brute: so off we started with our prisoner.

We arrived in camp just in time to report the result of our expedition to the commanding officer, who was much amused at our bringing, in addition to an ample supply of forage, etc., an impertinent fellow, with his head tied up in a bag. The next morning, after a severe lecture, our prisoner received his *congé* [leave] and was desired to return home and tell his friends that we differed entirely from other soldiers who had occupied the country, for we paid ready money for everything we required and expected to be treated with civility by the inhabitants.

A few days afterwards, another foraging party was organised, and on their arrival at the same village every door was opened, and provisions, corn, hay, etc., offered in abundance, while the greatest civility was paid to our men. The proprietor of the inn was foremost in proffering his services, and expressed his regret for what had occurred before, stating that the cause of it was that, in the dark, the inhabitants mistaking us for a body of men belonging to the Spanish Army, had fled, as a party of soldiers belonging to that nation had a short time before robbed them of their pigs, poultry, and linen, and ill-treated their wives and daughters. After this, our soldiers, when on foraging expeditions, were ordered to dress in uniform, to show the country people that they belonged to the British Army.

⟡· The Passage Of The Adour

Immediately after the battle of Nivelle, Lord Wellington determined to advance his whole line on to French ground. The right, under his own command, pushed on towards Orthes, whilst the left, under the command of Sir John Hope, proceeded in the direction of Bayonne. We (the Guards) were incorporated in the latter *corps d'armée*.

Whilst these operations were going on, Soult was organising his discouraged army, in order to make, as early as possible, another convenient stand. The enemy fell back on Orthes, and there took up a strong position. Soult was, nevertheless, destined to be beaten again at Orthes.

I must here record an incident which created a considerable sensation in military circles in connexion with the battle of Orthes. The 10th Hussars, officered exclusively by men belonging to the noblest families of Great Britain, showed a desire to take a more active part in the contest than their colonel (Quintin) thought prudent. They pressed hard to be permitted to charge the French cavalry on more than one occasion but in vain. This so disgusted every officer in the regiment, that they eventually signed a *round robin,* by which they agreed never again to speak to their colonel. When the regiment returned to England, a court of inquiry was held, which resulted, through the protection of the Prince Regent, in the colonel's exoneration from all blame, and at the same time the exchange of the rebellious officers into other regiments.[20]

---

20 Sir George Augustus Quentin (1760–1853), colonel of the 10th Hussars, later followed one of his detractors, Colonel Charles Palmer, to Paris in order to challenge him to a duel: according to John Mollo, in *The Prince's Dolls,* 'At twelve paces Quentin, as the aggrieved party, fired first but missed, whereupon Palmer ... fired into the air ... the affair ended and the parties returned to Paris.'

Lord Wellington had determined to cross the Adour, and Sir John Hope was entrusted with a *corps d'armée,* which was the first to perform this difficult operation. It was necessary to provide Sir John Hope with a number of small boats, these were accordingly brought on the backs of mules from various Spanish ports, it being impossible, on account of the surf at the entrance of the Adour, as well as the command which the French held of that river, for Lord Wellington to avail himself of water carriage. Soult had given orders for the forces under General Thevenot to dispute the passage.

The first operations of our corps were to throw over the 3rd Guards, under the command of the gallant Colonel Stopford. This was not accomplished without much difficulty, but it was imperatively necessary, in order to protect the point where the construction of the bridge of boats would terminate. They had not been long on the French side of the river before a considerable body of men were seen issuing from Bayonne. Sir John Hope ordered our artillery and rockets[21] then for the first time employed, to support our small band. Three or four regiments of French infantry were approaching rapidly, when a well-directed fire of rockets fell amongst them. The consternation of the Frenchmen was such, when these hissing, serpent-like projectiles descended, that a panic ensued, and they retreated upon Bayonne. The next day the bridge of boats was completed, and the whole Army crossed.

Bayonne was eventually invested after a contest, in which it was supposed our loss exceeded 500 or 600 men. Here we remained in camp about six weeks, expecting to besiege the citadel, but this event never came off. We, however, met with a severe disaster and a reverse. The enemy made an unexpected sortie, and surrounded General Sir John Hope, when

21 A variety of rockets, named after their inventor, William Congreve, were employed by the British Army during the period – they could be fired vertically from a 'firing frame' or horizontally at ground level: either way, their effect was more psychological than material. Wellington remained scornful of their use but they were successfully employed on a number of occasions, most particularly at Leipzig in 1813 when a troop was attached to the Allied armies.

he and the whole of his staff were taken prisoners.[22] Among the many officers of the Guards who were taken prisoners in the unfortunate sortie was the Honourable H. Townshend, commonly called Bull Townshend. He was celebrated as a *bon vivant*, and in consequence of his too great indulgence in the pleasures of the table, had become very unwieldy and could not move quick enough to please his nimble captors: so he received many prods in the back from a sharp bayonet. After repeated threats, however, he was dismissed with what our American friends would be pleased to designate 'a severe booting'. The late Sir Willoughby Cotton was also a prisoner. It really seemed as if the enemy had made choice of our fattest officers. Sir Willoughby escaped by giving up his watch and all the money which he had in his pockets, but this consisting of a Spanish dollar only, the smallness of the sum subjected him to the same ignominious treatment as had been experienced by Townshend.

The hardly-contested battle of Toulouse was fought about this period, but the Guards were not present to share the honours of a contest which closed the eventful war of the Spanish Peninsula.[23]

🐾· London Society

In the year 1814 my battalion of the Guards was once more in its old quarters in Portman Street barracks, enjoying the fame of our Spanish campaign. Good society at the period to which I refer was, to use a familiar expression, wonderfully *select*. At the present time one can hardly conceive the importance which was attached to getting admittance to Almack's,[24] the seventh heaven of the fashionable world. Of the 300 officers of the Foot Guards, not more than half a dozen were honoured

---

22 Launched on 14th April 1814, in ignorance of Napoleon's abdication eight days earlier, the besieged French garrison surprised their British foes in a night-raid, killing General Hay, their commander, and causing much panic, before being driven back by the Brigade of Foot Guards.

23 Toulouse was fought on 10th April 1814, thus making the above-mentioned sortie from Bayonne the final action of the Peninsular War.

24 William Almack's fashionable assembly rooms, designed by Robert Mylne in 1765, and situated in King Street, St James's.

with vouchers of admission to this exclusive temple of the *beau monde*, the gates of which were guarded by lady patronesses, whose smiles or frowns consigned men and women to happiness or despair. These lady patronesses were the Ladies Castlereagh, Jersey, Cowper, and Sefton, Mrs Drummond Burrell – now Lady Willoughby – the Princess Esterhazy, and the Countess Lieven.

The most popular amongst these *grandes dames* was unquestionably Lady Cowper, now Lady Palmerston. Lady Jersey's bearing, on the contrary, was that of a theatrical tragedy queen, and whilst attempting the sublime, she frequently made herself simply ridiculous: being inconceivably rude and in her manner often ill-bred. Lady Sefton was kind and amiable, Madame de Lieven haughty and exclusive,[25] Princess Esterhazy was a *bon enfant*, Lady Castlereagh and Mrs Burrell *des très grandes dames*.

Many diplomatic arts, much finesse, and a host of intrigues, were set in motion to get an invitation to Almack's. Very often, persons whose rank and fortunes entitled them to the *entrée*, were excluded by the cliqueism of the lady patronesses: for the female government of Almack's was a pure despotism and subject to all the caprices of despotic rule. The fair ladies who ruled supreme over this little dancing and gossiping world issued a solemn proclamation that no gentleman should appear at the assemblies without being dressed in knee-breeches, white cravat, and *chapeau*. On one occasion, the Duke of Wellington was about to ascend the staircase of the ballroom dressed in black trousers, when the vigilant Mr Willis, the guardian of the establishment, stepped forward and said: 'Your Grace cannot be admitted in trousers,' whereupon the duke, who had a great respect for orders and regulations, quietly walked away.

The dandies of society were Beau Brummell (of whom I shall have to say something on another occasion), the Duke of Argyle, the Lords Worcester, Alvanley and Foley, Henry Pierrepoint, John Mills, Bradshaw, Henry de Ros, Charles Standish, Edward Montagu, Hervey Aston, Dan Mackinnon, George Dawson Damer, Lloyd (commonly known as Rufus

---

25 Dorothea Khristoforovna, Countess Lieven in the Russian nobility (1785–1857), was wife of the Russian ambassador and a renowned political hostess.

Lloyd), and others who have escaped my memory. They were great frequenters of White's Club in St James's Street, where, in the famous bay window, they mustered in force.

Drinking and play were more universally indulged in then than at the present time, and many men still living must remember the couple of bottles of port – at least – which accompanied his dinner in those days. Indeed, female society amongst the upper classes was most notoriously neglected: except, perhaps, by romantic foreigners, who were the heroes of many a fashionable adventure that fed the clubs with ever-acceptable scandal. How could it be otherwise, when husbands spent their days in the hunting-field, or were entirely occupied with politics and always away from home during the day, whilst the dinner-party, commencing at seven or eight, frequently did not break up before one in the morning? There were then four- and even five-bottle men, and the only thing that saved them was drinking very slowly and out of very small glasses. The learned head of the law, Lord Eldon, and his brother, Lord Stowell, used to say that they had drunk more bad port than any two men in England. Indeed, the former was rather apt to be overtaken and to speak occasionally somewhat thicker than natural, after long and heavy potations. The late Lords Panmure, Dufferin, and Blayney, wonderful to relate, were six-bottle men at this time, and I really think that if the good society of 1815 could appear before their more moderate descendants in the state they were generally reduced to after dinner, the moderns would pronounce their ancestors fit for nothing but bed.

⤜· Hyde Park After The War

That extensive district of park land, the entrances of which are in Piccadilly and Oxford Street, was far more rural in appearance in 1815 than at the present day. Under the trees cows and deer were grazing, the paths were fewer and none told of that perpetual tread of human feet which now destroys all idea of country charms and illusions. As you gazed from an eminence, no rows of monotonous houses reminded you of the vicinity of a large city, and the atmosphere of Hyde Park was then much more like what God had made it than the hazy, grey, coal-darkened, half-twilight of the

London of today. The company which then congregated daily, about five, was composed of dandies and women in the best society, the men mounted on such horses as England alone could then produce. The dandy's dress consisted of a blue coat with brass buttons, leather breeches and top boots, and it was the fashion to wear a deep, stiff white cravat, which prevented you from seeing your boots while standing. All the world watched Brummell to imitate him and order their clothes of the tradesmen who dressed that sublime dandy. One day, a youthful beau approached Brummell and said, 'Permit me to ask you where you get your blacking?' 'Ah!' replied Brummell, gazing complacently at his boots, 'my blacking positively ruins me. I will tell you in confidence, it is made with the finest champagne!'

⋙· London Hotels

There was a class of men, of very high rank, such as Lords Wellington, Nelson, and Collingwood, Sir John Moore, and some few others, who never frequented the clubs. The persons to whom I refer and amongst whom were many members of the sporting world, used to congregate at a few hotels. The Clarendon, Limmer's, Ibbetson's, Fladong's, Stephens' and Grillon's, were the fashionable hotels. The Clarendon was then kept by a French cook, Jacquiers, who contrived to amass a large sum of money in the service of Louis XVIII in England and subsequently with Lord Darnley. This was the only public hotel where you could get a genuine French dinner and for which you seldom paid less than three or four pounds: your bottle of champagne or claret, in the year 1814, costing you a guinea.

Limmer's was an evening resort for all the sporting world. In fact, it was a midnight Tattersall's,[26] where you heard nothing but the language of the turf and where men with not very clean hands used to make up their books. Limmer's was the most dirty hotel in London but in the gloomy, comfortless coffee-room, might be seen many members of the rich squirearchy, who visited London during the sporting season. This hotel was so frequently crowded that a bed could not be obtained for any

---

26 Richard Tattersall's horse market at Hyde Park Corner was the principal meeting place and betting shop of the horse-racing fraternity.

amount of money: but you could always get a very good plain English dinner, an excellent bottle of port, and some famous gin-punch.

Ibbetson's hotel was chiefly patronised by the clergy and young men from the universities. The charges there were more economical than at similar establishments. Fladong's, in Oxford Street, was chiefly frequented by naval men, for in those days there was no club for sailors. Stephens', in Bond Street, was a fashionable hotel, supported by officers of the Army and men about town. If a stranger asked to dine there, he was stared at by the servants and very solemnly assured that there was no table vacant. It was not an uncommon thing to see thirty or forty saddle-horses and tilburies[27] waiting outside this hotel. I recollect two of my old Welsh friends, who used each of them to dispose of five bottles of wine daily, residing here in 1815, when the familiar joints, boiled fish, and fried soles, were the only eatables you could order.

🐾· London Clubs

The members of the clubs of London, many years since, were persons, almost without exception, belonging exclusively to the aristocratic world: 'My tradesmen,' as 'King' Allen used to call the bankers and the merchants, had not then invaded White's, Boodle's, Brooks's, or Wattier's, in Bolton Street, Piccadilly, which, with the Guards', Arthur's, and Graham's, were the only clubs at the West End of the town. White's was decidedly the most difficult of entry: its list of members comprised nearly all the noble names of Great Britain.

The politics of White's Club were then decidedly Tory. It was here that play was carried on to an extent which made many ravages in large fortunes, the traces of which have not disappeared at the present day. General Scott, the father-in-law of George Canning and the Duke of Portland, was known to have won at White's £200,000, thanks to his notorious sobriety and knowledge of the game of whist. The general possessed a great advantage over his companions by avoiding those indulgences at the table which used to muddle other men's brains. He confined himself to

27 Open, two-wheeled carriages.

dining off boiled chicken with toast and water. By such a regimen he came to the whist-table with a clear head and possessing as he did a remarkable memory, with great coolness and judgment, he was able honestly to win the enormous sum of £200,000.

At Brooks's, for nearly half a century, the play was of a more gambling nature than at White's. Faro and macao[28] were indulged in to an extent, which enabled a man to win or lose a considerable fortune in one night. Here Charles James Fox, Selwyn, Lord Carlisle, Lord Robert Spencer, General Fitzpatrick, and other great Whigs, won and lost hundreds of thousands, frequently remaining at the table for many hours without rising.

On one occasion, Lord Robert Spencer contrived to lose the last shilling of his considerable fortune, given him by his brother, the Duke of Marlborough. General Fitzpatrick being much in the same condition, they agreed to raise a sum of money in order that they might keep a faro bank. The members of the club made no objection and ere long they carried out their design. As is generally the case, the bank was a winner and Lord Robert bagged, as his share of the proceeds, £100,000. He retired, strange to say, from the fetid atmosphere of play with the money in his pocket and never again gambled. George Harley Drummond, of the famous banking-house, Charing Cross, only played once in his whole life at White's Club, at whist, on which occasion he lost £20,000 to Brummell. This event caused him to retire from the banking-house of which he was a partner.

Lord Carlisle was one of the most remarkable victims amongst the players at Brooks's and Charles Fox, his friend, was not more fortunate, being subsequently always in pecuniary difficulties. Many a time, after a long night of hard play, the loser found himself at the establishment of Howard and Gibbs, then the fashionable and patronised money-lenders. These gentlemen never failed to make hard terms with the borrower, although ample security was invariably demanded.

The Guards' Club was established for the three regiments of Foot Guards and was conducted upon a military system. Billiards and low whist

---

28 According to Hubert Cole, in *Beau Brummell*, macao was 'a form of vingt-et-un, calling for no particular skills but a steady nerve'.

were the only games indulged in. The dinner was, perhaps, better than at most clubs and considerably cheaper. I had the honour of being a member for several years, during which time I have nothing to remember but the most agreeable incidents. Arthur's and Graham's were less aristocratic than those I have mentioned. It was at the latter, thirty years ago, that a most painful circumstance took place. A nobleman of the highest position and influence in society was detected cheating at cards and after a trial, which did not terminate in his favour, he died of a broken heart.

Upon one occasion, some gentlemen of both White's and Brooks' had the honour to dine with the Prince Regent and during the conversation, the prince inquired what sort of dinners they got at their clubs: upon which Sir Thomas Stepney, one of the guests, observed that their dinners were always the same, 'The eternal joints, beefsteaks, the boiled fowl with oyster sauce and an apple tart. This is what we have, sir, at our clubs, and very monotonous fare it is!' The prince, without further remark, rang the bell for his cook, Wattier, and in the presence of those who dined at the royal table, asked him whether he would take a house and organise a dinner club. Wattier assented and named Madison, the prince's page, manager and Labourie the cook, from the royal kitchen. The club flourished only a few years, owing to the high play that was carried on there. The Duke of York patronised it and was a member. I was a member in 1816 and frequently saw His Royal Highness there. The dinners were exquisite: the best Parisian cooks could not beat Labourie. The favourite game played there was macao. Upon one occasion, Jack Bouverie, brother of Lady Heytesbury, was losing large sums and became very irritable. Raikes, with bad taste, laughed at Bouverie and attempted to amuse us with some of his stale jokes: upon which, Bouverie threw his play-bowl – with the few counters it contained – at Raikes's head. Unfortunately it struck him and made the city dandy angry – but no serious results followed this open insult.

PART

TWO

British soldiers on the streets of Paris. Gronow was part of the Allied contingent sent to occupy the French capital.

A HOT CORNER OF IT

'The cannibal has left his den ... The Corsican wolf has landed in the Bay of San Juan ... The tiger has arrived at Gay ... The wretch spent the night at Grenoble ... The tyrant has arrived at Lyons ... The usurper has been seen within fifty miles of Paris ... Bonaparte is advancing with great rapidity, but he will not set his foot inside the walls of Paris ... Tomorrow Napoleon will be at our gates ... The emperor has arrived at Fontainebleau ... His Imperial Majesty Napoleon entered Paris yesterday, surrounded by his loyal subjects ...'

Thus, in a nutshell, the Paris Moniteur *describes Napoleon's escape from Elba on 26th February 1815 and triumphant return to Paris and power on 20th March. But the 'Corsican wolf' had apparently turned into a lamb en route, for immediately on resuming his imperial throne, he let it be known that he desired peace. Indeed, a flurry of letters were sent to the sovereigns of Europe, assuring one and all that the emperor had no territorial ambitions and simply wanted a quiet life.*

No one was listening. In fact, before Bonaparte had reached Paris, the Allied Powers decreed him an outlaw and dubbed him 'the grand disturber of the peace of the world'. And a new coalition was formed to defeat – not France per se – but Napoleon himself. The crowned heads of a continent had lined up against a single person: the 'wolf', 'tiger', 'tyrant' and 'usurper', Napoleon Bonaparte. And this time they meant to finish the business – for good. Four separate armies were to be raised for a mighty march on Paris:

Russian, Austrian, Prussian, and Anglo-Dutch. The whole to be funded by British gold.

Napoleon could not afford to wait for this avalanche of men to engulf him. He was left with no choice but to fight for his crown: he simply had to take the initiative. According to Haythornthwaite, in Waterloo Men: 'his best hope of salvation was to take the offensive against the nearest Allied forces, and by securing a rapid victory, to establish a position from which he could negotiate with advantage.' The only Allied armies within striking distance were Wellington's and Blücher's, over the border in Belgium. Napoleon's plan, therefore, was to make a surprise thrust north-east, drive a wedge between Wellington and Blücher, defeat each of their armies in turn, and seize Brussels. If he could deliver this knock-out blow before the Austrian and Russian armies reached the Rhine, then perhaps the coalition would crumble and he could negotiate a favourable peace. The scheme was simple, brilliant, yet fraught with risk: but it constituted Napoleon's last throw of the dice.

On 15th June 1815 Napoleon and his Armée du Nord cross the Sambre into Belgium, catching the Allies completely off balance. The next day, he inflicted a crushing defeat on the Prussians at Ligny: but some ten miles to the north-east, at the crossroads of Quatre Bras, Wellington's Anglo-Netherlands force capitalised on shoddy French staff work, and beat off a lukewarm attack by Marshal Ney. Wellington then retreated to a prepared position at Mont St Jean and proposed to make a stand, providing the Prussians marched to his aid. The 72-year-old Blücher – beaten at Ligny and bruised from a fall from his horse – promised to help and the stage was set for the final showdown. Wellington set up his headquarters in a village five miles behind the battlefield, by the name of Waterloo.

And so, as David Chandler observes in his Dictionary of the Napoleonic Wars, 'Three days after crossing the Sambre onto Belgian territory, and two days after the battles of Quatre Bras against Wellington, and Ligny against Blücher, Napoleon fought and lost the most famous battle in modern history – Waterloo.'

'While the general outline of the battle of Waterloo is clear beyond dispute,' writes Harold T. Parker, in Three Napoleonic Battles, 'details of the sequence and timing of events and of responsibility for certain orders have been a subject of controversy among historians.' A theme taken up by Elizabeth Longford, who, in searching for some kind of order in the chaos of war, observed in her biography of Wellington that: 'There is something so ponderously classical about the battle of Waterloo that it comes as no surprise to find it unrolling in five acts.' Broadly speaking, the five phases of the battle were as follows: the sustained, yet ultimately abortive attacks on the Allied bastion at the château of Hougoumont by Jérôme Bonaparte, the emperor's brother; the abortive attack on Wellington's right-centre by d'Erlon's corps; the sustained yet fruitless attacks on Wellington's line by Ney's massed cavalry; the sustained and ultimately successful attack on Napoleon's right flank by Blücher's Prussians; and the abortive attack on Wellington's centre by the Imperial Guard, followed immediately by the collapse and rout of the French Army.

These phases, then, constitute the major episodes of the drama: though one should not forget the heroic – yet tragically doomed – charges of the British heavy cavalry; nor the equally heroic and equally doomed defence of the farmhouse of La Haie Sainte by the Hanoverians of the King's German Legion; nor the fact that throughout the whole day, the Allied line was subject to bombardment from the eighty guns of Napoleon's grand battery.

No one really knows how many died at Waterloo (Gronow's regiment, the 1st Foot Guards, lost over 1,000 men at Quatre Bras and Waterloo combined), but it is reasonable to suppose that by nightfall around 40,000 men and 10,000 horses lay dead or wounded on a field some three square miles in size. Yet despite the controversies of the battle, the consequences were clear: within fifty days Napoleon was on his way to final exile on the tiny South Atlantic island of St Helena, and the Bourbons – in the obese form of Louis XVIII – back on the throne of France.

The day after Waterloo, however, saw Gronow and the Guards – along with the rest of Wellington's troops – begin their march on Paris. It was interrupted on 26th June by the necessity of taking the fortified town of Péronne: a task entrusted to Sir John Byng and the Brigade of Guards, augmented by a Dutch-Belgian brigade. According to Hamilton's Origin and

History of the First or Grenadier Guards: 'The hornwork was carried with little loss, and a Dutch brigade of four nine-pounders being brought up and established to the east of the town, to take in reverse the face to be attacked, a few shots were exchanged; while a brigade of four field-pieces was placed so as to command the front of the hornwork itself. After a short interval General Byng sent forward Lieutenant Colonel Stanhope, his acting quartermaster general, with a flag of truce, upon which the garrison capitulated, and the maiden fortress surrendered to the Guards, on condition of the men being allowed to go to their homes.'

Two days later, with Paris a mere thirty-five miles distant, Gronow was promoted lieutenant and captain (the former being his 'Guards' rank, the latter his 'Line' rank). And on 7th July the Allies entered the capital at last, the British contingent camping in the Bois de Boulogne: 'The Guards were to have marched through the streets with laurels in their caps,' states Hamilton, 'but at the last moment the authorities directed them to march straight to the "Bois", a quiet way of entering the capital not at all appreciated by either officers or men.' The three-year occupation of Paris had begun.

❧

⊱· The Guards Marching From Enghien, June 1815

Two battalions of my regiment had started from Brussels. The other, the Second, to which I belonged, remained in London and I saw no prospect of taking part in the great events about to take place on the Continent.[1]

Early in June I had the honour of dining with Colonel Darling, the deputy adjutant-general, and I was there introduced to Sir Thomas Picton. He was very gracious, and on his two aides-de-camp (Major Tyler and my friend Chambers, of the Guards) lamenting that I was obliged to remain at home, Sir Thomas said, 'Is the lad really anxious to go out?' Chambers answered that it was the height of my ambition. Sir Thomas inquired if all

---

1   In fact, Gronow belonged to the First Battalion, and it was the Second and Third Battalions that had been deployed.

the appointments to his staff were filled up and then added with a grim smile: 'If Tyler is killed, which is not at all unlikely, I do not know why I should not take my countryman: he may go over with me if he can get leave.' I was overjoyed at this and after thanking the general a thousand times, made my bow and retired.

I was much elated at the thought of being Picton's aide-de-camp – though that somewhat remote contingency depended upon my friends Tyler or Chambers (or others) meeting with an untimely end – but at eighteen, *on ne doute de rien*.[2] So I set about thinking how I should manage to get my outfit, in order to appear at Brussels in a manner worthy of the aide-de-camp of the great general. As my funds were at a low ebb, I went to Cox and Greenwoods, those staunch friends of the hard-up soldier. Sailors may talk of the 'little cherub that sits up aloft,' but commend me for liberality, kindness, and generosity, to my old friends in Craig's Court. I there obtained £200, which I took with me to a gambling-house in St James's Square, where I managed, by some wonderful accident, to win £600, and having obtained the sinews of war, I made numerous purchases: amongst others, two first-rate horses at Tattersall's, for a high figure, which were embarked for Ostend, along with my groom. I had not got leave but thought I should get back, after the great battle that appeared imminent, in time to mount guard at St James's.

On a Saturday I accompanied Chambers in his carriage to Ramsgate, where Sir Thomas Picton and Tyler had already arrived. We remained there for the Sunday and embarked on Monday in a vessel that had been hired for the general and his suite. On the same day we arrived at Ostend and put up at a hotel in the square, where I was surprised to hear the general, in excellent French, get up a flirtation with our very pretty waiting-maid.

Sir Thomas was a stern-looking, strong-built man, about the middle height, and considered very like the Hetman Platov.[3] He generally wore a blue frock-coat – very tightly buttoned up to the throat – a large black

---

2 'One doubts nothing'. Both Picton and Chambers died at Waterloo; Tyler survived.

3 General Matvei Ivanovich Platov (1751–1818) was the colourful leader of Russia's Don Cossacks and much celebrated in England after Russia's defeat of Napoleon in 1812.

silk neckcloth, showing little or no shirt collar, dark trousers, boots, and a round hat. It was in this very dress that he was attired at Quatre Bras, as he hurried off to the scene of action before his uniform arrived.[4] After sleeping at Ostend, the general and Tyler went the next morning to Ghent and on Thursday to Brussels. I proceeded by boat to Ghent and without stopping, hired a carriage and arrived in time to order rooms for Sir Thomas at the Hôtel d'Angleterre, Rue de la Madeleine, at Brussels. Our horses followed us.

While we were at breakfast, Colonel Canning came to inform the general that the Duke of Wellington wished to see him immediately. Sir Thomas lost not a moment in obeying the order of his chief, leaving the breakfast table and proceeding to the park, where Wellington was walking with Fitzroy Somerset and the Duke of Richmond. Picton's manner was always more familiar than the duke liked in his lieutenants and on this occasion he approached him in a careless sort of way, just as he might have met an equal. The duke bowed coldly to him and said, 'I am glad you are come, Sir Thomas, the sooner you get on horseback the better: no time is to be lost. You will take command of the troops in advance. The Prince of Orange knows by this time that you will go to his assistance.' Picton appeared not to like the duke's manner, for when he bowed and left he muttered a few words, which convinced those who were there with him that he was not much pleased with his interview.

⇌· Quatre Bras

I got upon the best of my two horses and followed Picton and his staff to Quatre Bras at full speed. His division was already engaged

---

4   According to Captain Mercer of the Royal Horse Artillery, in his *Journal of the Waterloo Campaign*: 'A man of no very prepossessing appearance came rambling amongst our guns, and entered into conversation with me on the occurrences of the day; he was dressed in a shabby old drab greatcoat and rusty roundhat. I took him at the time for some amateur from Brussels, of whom we had heard there were several hovering about, and thinking many of his questions rather impertinent, I was somewhat short in answering them, and he soon left us. Great was my astonishment on learning soon after that this was Sir Thomas Picton.'

in supporting the Prince of Orange and had deployed itself in two lines in front of the road to Sombreffe when he arrived. Sir Thomas immediately took command. Shortly afterwards, Kempt's and Pack's brigades arrived by the Brussels road and part of Alten's division by the Nivelles road.

Ney was very strong in cavalry and our men were constantly formed into squares to receive them. The famous Kellermann – the hero of Marengo – tried a last charge and was very nearly taken or killed, as his horse was shot under him when very near us. Wellington at last took the offensive: a charge was made against the French, which succeeded, and we remained masters of the field. I acted as a mere spectator and got, on one occasion, just within twenty or thirty yards of some of the cuirassiers[5] but my horse was too quick for them.

On the 17th Wellington retreated upon Waterloo, about eleven o'clock. The infantry were masked by the cavalry in two lines, parallel to the Namur road. Our cavalry retired on the approach of the French cavalry, in three columns, on the Brussels road. A torrent of rain fell, upon the emperor's ordering the heavy cavalry to charge us; while the fire of sixty or eighty pieces of cannon showed that we had chosen our position at Waterloo. Chambers said to me, 'Now, Gronow, the loss has been very severe in the Guards[6] and I think you ought to go and see whether you are wanted. For, as you have really nothing to do with Picton, you had better join your regiment, or you may get into a scrape.' Taking his advice, I rode off to where the Guards were stationed. The officers (among whom I remember Colonel Thomas and Brigade-Major Miller) expressed their astonishment and amazement on seeing me and exclaimed, 'What the deuce brought you here? Why are you not with your battalion in London? Get off your horse and explain how you came here!'

---

5 A kind of 'heavy' cavalry, protected by steel helmets and breast-plates, the so-called 'cuirass', and mounted on large, powerful horses. They were used as shock troops on the battlefield.

6 The First Guards sustained over 500 casualties at Quatre Bras.

Things were beginning to look a little awkward when Gunthorpe, the adjutant (a great friend of mine), took my part and said, 'As he is here, let us make the most of him, there's plenty of work for everyone. Come, Gronow, you shall go with Captain Clements and a detachment to the village of Waterloo, to take charge of the French prisoners.' 'What the deuce shall I do with my horse?' I asked. Upon which Captain Stopford, aide-de-camp to Sir John Byng, volunteered to buy him. Having thus once more become a foot soldier, I started according to orders and arrived at Waterloo.

⇝· The Battle Of Waterloo

At daylight on the 18th we were agreeably surprised to see a detachment of the 3rd Guards – commanded by Captain Wigston and Ensign George Anson – who had been sent to relieve us. I took the opportunity of giving Anson (then a fine lad of seventeen) a silver watch made by Barwise, which his mother, Lady Anson, had requested me to take over to him. Bob Clements and I then proceeded to join our regiment.

The road was ankle-deep in mud and slough, and we had not proceeded a quarter of a mile when we heard the trampling of horses' feet, and on looking round perceived a large cavalcade of officers coming at full speed. In a moment we recognised the duke himself at their head. He was accompanied by the Duke of Richmond and his son, Lord William Lennox. The entire staff was close at hand: the Prince of Orange, Count Pozzo di Borgo, Baron Vincent, the Spanish General Alava, Prince Castel Cicala, with their several aides-de-camp; Felton Harvey, Fitzroy Somerset, and Delancey were the last that appeared. They all seemed as unconcerned as if they were riding to meet the hounds in some quiet English county.

In about half an hour we joined our comrades in camp, who were endeavouring to dry their accoutrements by the morning sun, after a night of rain and discomfort in their bivouac. I was now greeted by many of my old friends with loud cries of 'How are you, old fellow? Take a glass of wine and a bit of ham? It will be perhaps your last breakfast.' Then Burges called out, 'Come here Gronow and tell us some London news!'

He had made himself a sort of gypsy tent with the aid of some blankets, a sergeant's halberd and a couple of muskets. My dear old friend was sitting upon a knapsack with Colonel Stuart (who afterwards lost an arm), eating cold pie and drinking champagne, which his servant had just brought from Brussels. I was not sorry to partake of his hospitality and after talking together some time, we were aroused by the drums beating to arms. We fell in and the muster-roll having been called, the piling of arms followed, but we were not allowed to leave our places.

The position taken up by the British Army was an excellent one: it was a sort of ridge, very favourable for artillery, and from which all the movements of the French could be discerned. In case of any disaster, Wellington had several roads in his rear by which a masterly retreat could have been effected through the forest on Brussels, but our glorious commander thought little about retreating: on the contrary, he set all his energies to work and determined to win the day.

Our brigade was under the orders of General Maitland and our division was commanded by Sir George Cooke. We occupied the right centre of the British line and had the château of Hougoumont at about a quarter of a mile's distance on our right. Picton was on the extreme left at La Haye Sainte with his division of two British and one Hanoverian brigades. Hougoumont was garrisoned by the 2nd and 3rd Regiments of Guards, a battalion of Germans and two battalions of artillery, who occupied the château and gardens. Between each regiment was a battery of guns and nearly the whole of the cavalry was to the left of Picton's division.

About half past eleven the bands of several French regiments were distinctly heard and soon after the French artillery opened fire. The rapid beating of the *pas de charge,* which I had often heard in Spain and which few men, however brave they may be, can listen to without a somewhat unpleasant sensation, announced that the enemy's columns were fast approaching. On our side the most profound silence prevailed, whilst the French, on the contrary, raised loud shouts and we heard the cry, *Vive l'Empereur!* from one end of their line to the other.

The battle commenced by the French throwing out clouds of skirmishers from Hougoumont to La Haye Sainte. Jérôme Bonaparte's division, supported by those of Foy and Bachelu, attacked Hougoumont: the wood and garden of which were taken and retaken several times, but after prodigies of valour performed on both sides, remained in the hands of the French who, however, sustained immense loss and the château still belonged to the invincible English Guards.[7]

Whilst the battle was raging in the wood and orchard, eighty French guns (mostly twelve-pounders) opened upon us and caused a heavy loss in our ranks. At the same moment we could perceive from our elevated position that the enemy were attacking La Haye Sainte in great force. At about two o'clock, Ney, with the I Corps formed in four columns, advanced *en echelon,* the left wing forward. They completely defeated and put to flight a Dutch-Belgian brigade and then attacked Picton's division.[8] He, however, made a desperate resistance and charged them several times, though they were four times his number. It was then that noble soldier was killed by a musket ball.[9] Things looked ill there, when the duke ordered up Adam's brigade, which regained the ground and eagerly pushed forward.

At the same time Lord Uxbridge commanded the cavalry to charge. This order was admirably executed by Somerset on one side and by Ponsonby on the other, and was for a time completely successful. The French infantry brigades of Quiot, Donzelot and Marcognet were rolled

---

7 Apart from the British Foot Guards, a significant number of Germans from the King's German Legion, the 1st and 3rd Hanoverian Brigades, and the 2nd Nassau Brigade, helped defend Hougoumont or support its garrison: a total force of over 7,000 men, aided by some forty-two guns from several batteries.

8 The Netherlanders of van Bijlandt's Brigade have been much maligned by the British: but some Belgian sources assert that these troops were ordered to retire from their exposed position in advance of Wellington's firing line before the French attack went in; and according to Boulger, in *The Belgians At Waterloo*: 'It is ... clear from the evidence that the Bijlandt brigade was withdrawn from the ground which under a mistaken view of the facts it was denounced for having abandoned.'

9 Picton, yelling, 'Charge! Charge! Hurrah!' was struck in the temple by a bullet and fell dead on his horse.

up and almost annihilated: twenty guns were dismantled or spiked[10] and many hundreds of prisoners taken – several squadrons of cuirassiers were also charged and put to the rout. Unfortunately, our cavalry went too far without proper supports and were charged and driven back by Milhaud's heavy cavalry and Jacquinot's lancers, and had to take refuge behind our own lines. Ney now received orders to attack La Haye Sainte, which was taken about four o'clock.[11] At the same hour Bülow's first columns made their appearance and attacked d'Erlon and Lobau.

The Guards had what in modern battues[12] is called a hot corner of it, and the greatest gluttons (and we had many such) must have allowed, when night came on that they had had fighting enough. I confess I am to this day astonished that any of us remained alive. From eleven o'clock till seven we were pounded with shot and shell at long and short range, were incessantly potted at by *tirailleurs* [sharpshooters] – who kept up a most biting fire – constantly charged by immense masses of cavalry, who seemed determined to go in and win (preceded as their visits were by a terrific fire of artillery), and last of all, we were attacked by *La Vieille Garde* itself. But here we came to the end of our long and fiery ordeal. The French veterans, conspicuous by their high bearskin caps and lofty stature, on breasting the ridge behind which we were at that time, were met by a fearful fire of artillery and musketry, which swept away whole masses of those valiant soldiers, and while in disorder, they were charged by us with complete success and driven in utter rout and discomfiture down the ravine. The Prussians having now arrived in force on the French right, a general advance of the whole line was ordered and the day was won.

---

10 Spiking a gun involved hammering a steel pin or 'spike' into the vent at the rear of the barrel. Only one gun – on either side – was known to have been disabled in this way at Waterloo, and it was done by a conscientious sergeant in Major Rogers' battery during D'Erlon's attack. The spike was later drilled out and the gun returned to action.

11 Other accounts suggest the farmhouse fell some time after six p.m., when the garrison's ammunition ran out.

12 Turkey-shoots or game hunts.

During the battle our squares presented a shocking sight. Inside we were nearly suffocated by the smoke and smell from burnt cartridges. It was impossible to move a yard without treading upon a wounded comrade or upon the bodies of the dead, and the loud groans of the wounded and dying were most appalling.

At four o'clock our square was a perfect hospital: being full of dead, dying, and mutilated soldiers. The charges of cavalry were in appearance very formidable, but in reality a great relief, as the artillery could no longer fire on us. The very earth shook under the enormous mass of men and horses. I shall never forget the strange noises our bullets made against the breastplates of Kellermann's and Milhaud's cuirassiers, 6,000–7,000 in number, who attacked us with great fury. I can only compare it (with a somewhat homely simile) to the noise of a violent hailstorm beating upon panes of glass.[13]

The artillery did great execution, but our musketry did not at first seem to kill many men, though it brought down a large number of horses and created indescribable confusion. The horses of the first rank of cuirassiers, in spite of all the efforts of their riders, came to a standstill, shaking and covered in foam, at about twenty yards' distance from our squares and generally resisted all attempts to force them to charge the line of serried steel. On one occasion, two gallant French officers forced their way into a gap momentarily created by the discharge of artillery: one was killed by Staples,[14] the other by Adair. Nothing could be more gallant than the behaviour of those veterans, many of whom had distinguished themselves on half the battlefields of Europe.

In the midst of our terrible fire, their officers were seen as if on parade, keeping order in their ranks, and encouraging them. Unable to renew the charge but unwilling to retreat, they brandished their swords with loud

---

13 Around four p.m. some 5,000 sabres from a mixture of cavalry units, not just cuirassiers, charged up the plateau to find the Allied infantry formed in twenty squares: an hour later, almost twice this number of French horsemen were engaged, and perhaps as many as twelve separate charges were made in total.

14 Presumably Gronow means Captain Edward Stables, who was later killed in the battle.

cries of *Vive l'Empereur!* and allowed themselves to be mowed down by hundreds rather than yield. Our men, who shot them down, could not help admiring the gallant bearing and heroic resignation of their enemies.

⨠• French Cavalry Charging The Brunswickers

Soon after the cuirassiers had retired, we observed the red hussars of the Garde Impériale charging a square of Brunswick riflemen,[15] who were about fifty yards from us. This charge was brilliantly executed but the well-sustained fire from the square baffled the enemy, who were obliged to retire after suffering a severe loss in killed and wounded. The ground was completely covered with those brave men, who lay in various positions, mutilated in every conceivable way. Among the fallen we perceived the gallant colonel of the hussars lying under his horse, which had been killed. All of a sudden two riflemen of the Brunswickers left their battalion and after taking from their hapless victim his purse, watch, and other articles of value, they deliberately put the colonel's pistols to the poor fellow's head and blew out his brains. 'Shame! shame!' was heard from our ranks and a feeling of indignation ran through the whole line, but the deed was done: this brave soldier lay a lifeless corpse in sight of his cruel foes, whose only excuse – perhaps – was that their sovereign, the Duke of Brunswick, had been killed two days before by the French.

Again and again various cavalry regiments – heavy dragoons, lancers, hussars, carabiniers of the Guard – endeavoured to break our walls of steel. The enemy's cavalry had to advance over ground which was so heavy that they could not reach us except at a trot: they therefore came upon us in a much more compact mass than they probably would have done if the ground had been more favourable. When they got within ten or fifteen yards they discharged their carbines, to the cry of *Vive l'Empereur!* but their fire produced little effect, as is generally the case with the fire of cavalry. Our men had orders not to fire unless they could do so on a near mass: the object being to economise our ammunition and not to waste it on scattered soldiers. The result was, that when the cavalry had discharged their

---

15 A corps of Germans raised by theDuke of Brunswick, who was killed at Quatre Bras.

carbines, and were still far off, we occasionally stood face to face, looking at each other inactively, not knowing what the next move might be.

When we received cavalry, the order was to fire low, so that on the first discharge of musketry, the ground was strewed with the fallen horses and their riders, which impeded the advance of those behind them and broke the shock of the charge. It was pitiable to witness the agony of the poor horses, which really seemed conscious of the dangers that surrounded them. We often saw a poor wounded animal raise its head, as if looking for its rider to afford him aid. There is nothing, perhaps, amongst the episodes of a great battle more striking than the débris of a cavalry charge, where men and horses are seen scattered and wounded on the ground in every variety of painful attitude. Many a time the heart sickened at the moaning tones of agony which came from man – and scarcely less intelligent horse – as they lay upon the field of battle.

🖎· The Unfortunate Charge Of The Household Brigade

When Lord Uxbridge gave orders to Sir W. Ponsonby and Lord Edward Somerset to charge the enemy, our cavalry advanced with the greatest bravery, cut through everything in their way, and gallantly attacked whole regiments of infantry. But eventually they came upon a masked battery of twenty guns, which carried death and destruction through our ranks and our poor fellows were obliged to give way. The French cavalry followed on their retreat when, perhaps, the severest hand-to-hand cavalry fighting took place within the memory of man. The Duke of Wellington was perfectly furious that this arm had been engaged without his orders and lost not a moment in sending them to the rear, where they remained during the rest of the day.[16] This disaster gave the French cavalry an opportunity of

---

16 Henry William Paget, or Lord Uxbridge, had been on frosty terms with Wellington for years, having eloped with the wife of Henry Wellesley, the duke's brother. After the fatal charge of the British heavy cavalry, Wellington apparently accosted Uxbridge with: 'Well, Paget, I hope you are satisfied with your cavalry now.' Uxbridge later declared that Wellington had simply given him complete control of the Allied cavalry: 'These are all the orders I ever received from the duke during this short campaign.'

annoying and insulting us and compelled the artillerymen to seek shelter in our squares, and if the French had been provided with tackle or harness of any description, our guns would have been taken. It is, therefore, not to be wondered that the duke should have expressed himself in no measured terms about the cavalry movements referred to. I recollect that our soldiers were so mortified at seeing the French deliberately walking their horses between our regiment and those to our right and left, that they shouted, 'Where are our cavalry? Why don't they come and pitch into those French fellows?'

➥· The Duke Of Wellington In Our Square
About four p.m. the enemy's artillery in front of us ceased firing all of a sudden and we saw large masses of cavalry advance. Not a man present who survived could have forgotten in after life the awful grandeur of that charge. You perceived at a distance what appeared to be an overwhelming, long moving line, which, ever advancing, glittered like a stormy wave when it catches the sunlight. On came the mounted host until they got near enough, whilst the very earth seemed to vibrate beneath their thundering tramp. One might suppose that nothing could have resisted the shock of this terrible moving mass. They were the famous cuirassiers, almost all old soldiers who had distinguished themselves on most of the battlefields of Europe. In an almost incredibly short period they were within twenty yards of us, shouting, *Vive l'Empereur!* The word of command, 'Prepare to receive cavalry!' had been given, every man in the front ranks knelt and a wall bristling with steel presented itself to the infuriated cuirassiers.

I should observe that just before this charge the duke entered by one of the angles of the square, accompanied only by one aide-de-camp: all the rest of his staff being either killed or wounded.[17] Our commander-in-chief, as far as I could judge, appeared perfectly composed, but looked very thoughtful and pale. He was dressed in a grey greatcoat with a cape, white cravat, leather pantaloons, Hessian boots, and a large cocked hat *à la Russe.*

---

17 Wellington employed eight ADCs at Waterloo: all but one were either killed or wounded, the lucky escapee being Major the Hon. Henry Percy.

The charge of the French cavalry was gallantly executed but our well-directed fire brought men and horses down, and ere long the utmost confusion arose in their ranks. The officers were exceedingly brave and by their gestures and fearless bearing did all in their power to encourage their men to form again and renew the attack. The duke sat unmoved, mounted on his favourite charger.[18] I recollect his asking Colonel Stanhope what o'clock it was, upon which Stanhope took out his watch and said it was twenty minutes past four. The duke replied, 'The battle is mine, and if the Prussians arrive soon there will be an end of the war.'

🐎· The Last Charge At Waterloo

It was about five o'clock on that memorable day that we suddenly received orders to retire behind an elevation in our rear. The enemy's artillery had come up *en masse* within 100 yards of us. By the time they began to discharge their guns, however, we were lying down behind the rising ground and protected by the ridge before referred to. The enemy's cavalry was in the rear of their artillery, in order to be ready to protect it if attacked – but no attempt was made on our part to do so. After they had pounded away at us for about half an hour, they deployed, and up came the whole mass of the infantry of the *Garde,* led on by the emperor in person. We had now before us probably about 20,000 of the best soldiers in France, the heroes of many memorable victories.[19] We saw the bearskin caps rising higher and higher, as they ascended the ridge of ground which separated us, and advanced nearer and nearer to our lines.

---

18 According to Andrew Roberts, in *Napoleon & Wellington*: 'Wellington's charger Copenhagen – a chestnut brown horse – carried him throughout the day' – the horse was named in honour of Nelson's famous victory of 1801.

19 Napoleon had three divisions of Imperial Guard infantry at Waterloo, each made up of four regiments, numbered 1 to 4. The Young Guard Division became embroiled in the battle for Plancenoit with von Bülow's Prussians, leaving two remaining divisions: one of four regiments of Chasseurs (1 to 4) and one of four regiments of Grenadiers (1 to 4). The units deployed in the evening attack on Wellington's line appear to have been the 3rd and 4th regiments of both these divisions combined, some 3,587 men in total. Some of these units were newly raised but the men in the ranks were veterans.

It was at this moment that the Duke of Wellington gave his famous order for our bayonet charge as he rode along the line. These are the precise words he made use of: 'Guards, get up and charge!' We were instantly on our legs and after so many hours of inaction and irritation at maintaining a purely defensive attitude (all the time suffering the loss of comrades and friends), the spirit which animated officers and men may easily be imagined. After firing a volley as soon as the enemy were within shot, we rushed on with fixed bayonets and that hearty *Hurrah!* peculiar to British soldiers.

It appeared that our men, deliberately and with calculation, singled out their victims, for as they came upon the Imperial Guard our line broke and the fighting became irregular. The impetuosity of our men seemed almost to paralyse their enemies: I witnessed several of the Imperial Guard who were run through the body apparently without any resistance on their part. I observed a big Welshman by the name of Hughes, who was six feet seven inches, run through with his bayonet and knock down with the butt-end of his firelock, I should think a dozen, at least, of his opponents. This terrible contest did not last more than ten minutes, for the Imperial Guard were soon in full retreat, leaving all their guns and many prisoners in our hands.

The famous General Cambronne was taken prisoner fighting hand-to-hand with the gallant Sir Colin Halkett, who was shortly after shot through the cheeks by a grapeshot. Cambronne's supposed answer of '*La Garde ne se rend pas*' was an invention of aftertimes and he himself always denied having used such an expression.[20]

---

20 General Pierre Jacques Cambronne (1770–1842) was a hard-fighting, hard-talking soldier from a poor background. He commanded the 1st Regiment of Chasseurs à Pied in Morand's Division, some 1,207 men in total. When his command was reduced to a single battalion at the close of battle, he arranged his troops in a triangle, two ranks deep, and continued to fire in retreat, while the rest of Napoleon's army bolted. Summoned to surrender by the British, he is supposed to have answered: 'The Guard dies, but does not surrender' and this is on his tombstone. In truth, however, he probably uttered a simple '*Merde!*' ('Shit!') Wellington, for one, never believed the heroic and somewhat poetic aphorism: 'Never, certainly, was anything so absurd as ascribing that saying to Cambronne. Why, I found him that evening in my room at Waterloo – him and General Mouton – and I bowed them out ... I would not let them sup with me that night. I thought they had behaved so very ill to the King of France.'

🐊· Meeting Of Wellington And Blücher

After our final charge and the retreat of the French Army we arrived and bivouacked about nine o'clock in the orchard of the farm of La Belle Alliance, about 100 yards from the farmhouse where Napoleon had remained for some hours. We were presently disturbed by the sound of trumpets. I immediately hurried off, in company with several other officers and found that the sound proceeded from a Prussian cavalry regiment with Blücher at its head. The Duke of Wellington, who had given rendezvous to Blücher at this spot, then rode up and the two victorious generals shook hands in the most cordial and hearty manner. After a short conversation our chief rode off to Brussels,[21] while Blücher and the Prussians joined their own army, which under General Gneisenau, was already in hot pursuit of the French. After this I entered the farmhouse where Napoleon had passed part of the day. The furniture had to all appearance been destroyed, but I found an immense fire made of a wooden bedstead and the legs of chairs, which appeared by the embers to have been burning a considerable time.

🐊· Sufferings Of The Wounded

On the following morning we had not advanced for many minutes before we met several of our gallant companions in arms who had been wounded. They were lying in wagons of the country and had been abandoned by the drivers. Some of these poor fellows belonged to our regiment and on passing close to one of the wagons a man cried out, 'For God's sake, Mr Gronow, give us some water or we shall go mad.' I did not hesitate for a moment but jumped into the cart and gave the poor fellow all the water my flask contained. The other wounded soldiers then entreated me to fill it with some muddy water, which they had descried in a neighbouring ditch, half filled by the rain of the preceding day. As I thought a flask would be of little use among so many, I took off my shako and having

---

21 In fact, Wellington took a slow ride back to his headquarters at the village of Waterloo, some five miles from the battlefield, and left for Brussels the following day.

first stopped up with my belcher handkerchief a hole that a musket ball had made in the top of it, filled it with water several times for these poor fellows, who were all too severely wounded to have got it for themselves and who drank it off with tears of delight.

⋙ • Shaving In A Minute

About twelve o'clock, on the second day after the battle of Waterloo, when on our march to Paris, we were ordered to come to a halt. Every officer and soldier immediately set to work to get rid of the superabundance of beard that had been suffered to grow for several days. During this not very agreeable duty, a shout was heard from Lord Saltoun, who called us to witness a bet he had made with Bob Ellison, that he, Ellison, could not shave off his beard in one minute.

Preparations were made, Ellison taking care to bathe his face for a considerable time in water. He then commenced operations and in less than a minute – and without the aid of a looking-glass – actually won his bet (a considerable one), to the astonishment and I must add, the satisfaction of his comrades. This feat appeared to us all perfectly impossible to accomplish, as his face was covered with the stubble of a week's growth of hair, so dark, that it had procured for him in the regiment the sobriquet of 'Black Bob'.

Ellison was one of our best officers. After joining the Brigade at Cadiz, he was present in every action in the Peninsula and was with the Light Companies at Hougoumont. He greatly distinguished himself there and on one occasion, when he was forced to retreat from the orchard to the château, he would have been bayoneted by the French, had not the men – with whom he was a great favourite – charged back and saved his life. Ellison led the storming party at Péronne and commanded the Second Battalion of his regiment in Canada. He was colonel of his old battalion in 1843 when, at a brigade field day in Hyde Park, on the occasion of a general salute, as he gave the word, 'Present arms!' he dropped down dead from his horse, while the old corps, in which he had passed nearly forty years, were presenting arms to him.

⤟· Péronne La Pucelle

The fourth or fifth day after Waterloo we arrived before Péronne La Pucelle[22] – the Virgin Town – as the inhabitants delighted to call it: for they boasted that it had never been taken by an enemy. The Duke of Wellington suddenly made his appearance in our bivouac and gave orders that we should, at all risks, take Péronne before night. We accordingly prepared for action and commenced proceedings by battering the gates with a strong fire of artillery. The guns of the virgin fortress returned the compliment and the first shot from the town fell under the belly of the duke's horse – but beyond knocking the gravel and stones about in all directions, did no injury.

The garrison consisted of 1,500 National Guards, who had sworn never to surrender to mortal man: but when these ardent volunteers saw our red coats coming in with a rush (and with a grim determination to take no denial) they wisely laid down their arms and capitulated. Our loss, on this occasion, amounted to nine killed and thirty wounded. Lord Saltoun had a narrow escape: a ball struck him on his breeches pocket, where half a dozen five-franc pieces broke the force of the blow. Saltoun, though not very Bonapartist in his opinions, retained the mark of the emperor's effigy on his thigh for some time, and though not returned as wounded, suffered great pain for several days after.[23]

⤟· Væ Victis[24]

On the Guards arriving at St Pont Maixans, a town situated about forty miles from Paris, I was sent by the adjutant to look out for quarters for myself and servant. In the neighbourhood of a small wood I perceived

---

22 It was 26th June according to Hamilton's *Origin and History of the First or Grenadier Guards*.

23 According to Hamilton: 'Saltoun immediately rushed to the assault with his light companies, which experienced some slight loss as they crossed the ditch, while Saltoun himself was struck by a grape shot as he was mounting the scaling ladder, but fortunately the shot, striking a purse full of coins, in his pocket, lessened the blow ... and he refused to report himself wounded.'

24 Woe to the victor.

a mill and near it a river, and on looking a little further, saw a large farmhouse: this I entered but could not discover any living being. My servant, however, who had gone upstairs, informed me that the farmer was lying in bed dreadfully wounded from numerous sabre cuts. I approached his bed and he appeared more dead than alive: but on my questioning him, he said the Prussians had been there the night before, had violated and carried off his three daughters, had taken away his cart-horses and cattle, and because he had no money to give them, they had tied him to his bed and cut him with their swords across the shin bones and left him fainting from pain and loss of blood. After further inquiries, he told me that he thought some of the Prussians were still in the cellar, upon which, I ordered my batman to load his musket, struck a light, and with a lantern proceeded to the cellar, where we found a Prussian soldier drunk and lying in a pool of wine, which had escaped from the casks he and his comrades had tapped. Upon seeing us he (with an oath in German) made a thrust at my batman with his sabre, which was parried. In an instant we bound the ruffian and brought him at the point of the bayonet into the presence of the poor farmer, who recognised him as one of the men who had outraged his unfortunate daughters and who afterwards wounded him. We carried our prisoner to the provost-sergeant, who, in his turn, took him to the Prussian headquarters where he was instantly shot.

⟫• Appearance Of Paris When The Allies Entered

I propose giving my own impression of the aspect of Paris and its vicinity when our regiment entered that city on 25th June 1815.[25] I recollect we marched from the plain of St Denis, my battalion being about 500 strong, the survivors of the heroic fight of 18th June. We approached near enough to be within fire of the batteries of Montmartre and bivouacked for three weeks in the Bois de Boulogne. That now beautiful garden was, at the period to which I refer, a wild pathless wood, swampy and entirely

---

25 Gronow has confused the dates. According to Hamilton, the regiment entered Paris on 7th July and, as seen above, the Guards had not yet taken Péronne on 25th June.

neglected. The Prussians, who were in bivouac near us, amused themselves by doing as much damage as they could without any useful aim or object: they cut down the finest trees and set the wood on fire at several points. There were about 3,000 of the Guards then encamped in the wood and I should think about 10,000 Prussians. Our camp was not remarkable for its courtesy towards them: in fact, our intercourse was confined to the most ordinary demands of duty, as allies in an enemy's country.

I believe I was one of the first of the British Army who penetrated into the heart of Paris after Waterloo. I entered by Porte Maillot and passed the Arc de Triomphe, which was then building. In those days the Champs Élysée only contained a few scattered houses and the roads were ankle-deep in mud. The only attempt at lighting was the suspension of a few lamps on cords, which crossed the roads. Here I found the Scotch regiments bivouacking; their peculiar uniform created a considerable sensation amongst the Parisian women, who did not hesitate to declare that the want of *culottes* was most indecent. I passed through their camp and proceeded on towards the gardens of the Tuileries. This ancient palace of the kings of France presented, so far as the old front is concerned, the same aspect that it does at the present day, but there were then no flower gardens – although the same stately rows of trees which now ornament the grounds were then in their midsummer verdure.

Being in uniform, I created an immense amount of curiosity amongst the Parisians who, by the way, I fancied regarded me with no loving looks. The first house I entered was a café in the garden of the Tuileries called 'Legac's'. I there met a man who told me he was a descendant of an Englishman, though he had been born in Paris and really never quitted France. He approached me saying, 'Sir, I am delighted to see an English officer in Paris and you are the first I have yet met with.' He talked about the battle of Waterloo and gave me some useful directions concerning restaurants and cafés. Along the boulevards were handsome houses, isolated, with gardens interspersed, and the roads were bordered on both sides with stately, spreading trees: some of them probably 100 years old. There was but an imperfect pavement, the stepping stones of which were adapted to display the Parisian female ankle and boot in all their calculated coquetry, and the road showed nothing but mother earth, in the middle of which a dirty gutter served to convey the impurities of the city to the river. The people in the streets appeared sulky and stupefied: here and there I noticed groups of the higher classes evidently discussing the events of the moment.

How strange humanity would look in our day in the costume of the First Empire. The ladies wore very scanty and short skirts, which left little or no waist, their bonnets were of exaggerated proportions and protruded at least a foot from their faces, and they generally carried a fan. The men wore blue or black coats, which were baggily made and reached down to their ankles, their hats were enormously large and spread out at the top.

I dined the first day of my entrance into Paris at the Café Anglais, on the Boulevard des Italiens, where I found to my surprise several of my brother officers. I recollect the charge for the dinner was about one-third what it would be at the present day. I had a potage, fish (anything but fresh), and according to English predilections and taste, of course I ordered a beef-steak and *pommes de terre*. The wine, I thought, was sour. The dinner cost about two francs.

The theatres at this time – as may be easily imagined – were not very well attended. I recollect going to the Français, where I saw for the first time the famous Talma. There was but a scanty audience. In fact, all the best places in the house were empty.

It may be easily imagined that, at a moment like this, most of those who had a stake in the country were pondering over the great and real drama that was then taking place. Napoleon had fled to Rochefort, the wreck of his army had retreated beyond the Loire, no list of killed and wounded had appeared, and strange to say, the official journal of Paris had made out that the imperial army at Waterloo had gained a great victory. There were, nevertheless, hundreds of people in Paris who knew to the contrary and many were already aware that they had lost relations and friends in the great battle.

When we were in Paris we heard that Napoleon, on making his first observation with his glass, surrounded by his generals, on the morning of the 18th, had said with an air of exultation on finding that we had not retreated as he expected, *'Je les triens donc ces Anglais'.*[26] But was answered by General Foy, *'Sire, l'infanterie Anglaise en duel c'est le diable.'* [27] We also heard that Soult, on remonstrating upon the uselessness of charging our squares with cavalry, had been severely reprimanded and had undergone the biting and sarcastic remark from the emperor: *'Vous croyez Wellington un grand homme, Général, parce qu'il vous a battu.'* [28]

Louis XVIII arrived (as well as I can remember) at the Tuileries on 26th July 1815[29] and his reception by the Parisians was a singular illustration of the versatile character of the French nation, and the sudden and often inexplicable changes that take place in the feeling of the populace. When the Bourbon, in his old lumbering state-carriage, drove down the Boulevards, accompanied by the *Gardes du Corps,* the people in the streets and at the windows displayed the wildest joy, enthusiastically shouting, *Vive le Roi!* amidst the waving of hats and handkerchiefs, while white sheets or white rags were made to do the duty of a Bourbon banner. The king was dressed in a blue coat with a red collar, and wore also a white waistcoat and a cocked hat with a white cockade in it. His portly and good-natured appearance seemed to be appreciated by the crowd, whom he saluted with a benevolent smile. I should here mention that two great devotees of the Church sat opposite to the king on this memorable occasion. The *cortège* proceeded slowly down the Rue de la Paix until the Tuileries was reached, where a company of the Guards, together with a certain number of the *Garde Nationale* of Paris, were stationed.

It fell to my lot to be on duty the day after, when the Duke of Wellington and Lord Castlereagh arrived to pay their respects to the restored monarch. I happened to be in the Salle des Maréchaux when these illustrious

---

26 'Now I have them, these English.'

27 'Sire, in a close fight, the English infantry are the very devil.'

28 'You believe Wellington a great man, General, because he beat you.'

29 In fact, Louis was greeted at the gates of Paris on 8th July with the Comte de Chabrol-Volvic's famous words: 'A hundred days have passed since the fatal moment when Your Majesty left his capital …'

personages passed through that magnificent apartment. The respect paid to the Duke of Wellington on this occasion may be easily imagined, from the fact that a number of ladies of the highest rank (and of course partisans of the legitimate dynasty) formed an avenue through which the hero of Waterloo passed, exchanging with them courteous recognitions. The king was waiting in the grand reception apartment to receive the great British captain. The interview, I have every reason to believe, was not confined to the courtesies of the palace.

The position of the duke was a difficult one. In the first place, he had to curb the vindictive vandalism of Blücher and his army, who would have levelled the city of Paris to the ground if they could have done so; on the other hand, he had to practise a considerable amount of diplomacy towards the newly restored king. At the same time, the duke's powers from his own government were necessarily limited. A spirit of vindictiveness pervaded the restored Court against Napoleon and his adherents, which the duke constantly endeavoured to modify. I must not forget to give an illustration of this state of feeling. It was actually proposed by Talleyrand, Fouché, and some important ecclesiastics of the ultra-royalist party, to arrest and shoot the emperor Napoleon, who was then at Rochefort. So anxious were they to commit this criminal, inhuman, and cowardly act on an illustrious fallen enemy, who had made the arms of France glorious throughout Europe, that they suggested to the duke – who had command of the old wooden-armed semaphores – to employ the telegraph to order what I should have designated by no other name than the assassination of the Caesar of modern history.

⤳· Reception In London

I got leave to go to England to join my battalion after we had been in Paris about a fortnight, and I never shall forget the reception I met with as I dashed up in a chaise and four to the door of Fenton's Hotel in St James's Street. Very few men from the army had yet arrived in London and a mob of about 1,000 people gathered round the door as I got out in my old, weather-beaten uniform, shaking hands with me and uttering loud cheers. I also recollect the capital English dinner old James, the well-known waiter, had provided to celebrate my return. *'Ce sont beaux jours de la vie'* – few and far between in our chequered existence – and I confess that my memory wanders back to them with pleasure, and some regret, to think they can never more return.

PART

THREE

Some Prima Ballerinas and their gentlemen admirers at the Green Room at the Opera House (or King's Theatre).

THE RENDEZVOUS OF ALL IDLERS

Paris, when entered from the north, wrote Arthur Bryant, in The Age of
Elegance, *'wore a deserted, forlorn look … a labyrinth of high, crazy,
crumbling medieval houses with pointed roofs and fantastic gables shutting
out the sky. Down the centre of the narrow, villainously-paved roadways
trickled streams of stinking water. Overhead ancient lanterns, slung from
ropes, swayed in the wind …'*

*The first Allied commander on the scene was Marshal Blücher. He arrived
even before Louis XVIII and his ministers, and as E. F. Henderson states
in* Blücher and the Uprising of Prussia Against Napoleon, *the vengeful
Prussian 'had now a few days of glory in which he was practically ruler of
Paris. He laid on the city a contribution of 100,000,000 francs.' But Blücher's
reign as the king of Paris ended with the arrival of Louis XVIII – the man
'who had learned nothing, and forgotten nothing' – who, surrounded as he
was by 30,000 foreign troops, was destined to be the last French monarch
fortunate enough to die on his throne.*

*Obese and infirm (Private Wheeler of the 51st Foot described him as 'an old
bloated poltroon'), Louis brought with him his brother, the ultra-conservative
Comte d'Artois (the future Charles X) and 'a host of hungry folk, princes of the
blood royal, dukes, and noble dames': all bent on making France suffer for its
revolution, its republic, and its empire. As Gregor Dallas notes, in* 1815: The
Roads to Waterloo, *'They were turning the clocks back. It was the revenge of old
ruling classes, no longer capable of responding to the new destinies of Europe.'*

Yet when Louis made his formal entry into his capital in the second week of July 1815, he met such an ecstatic welcome that 'Wellington – amazed by the wild cheering – wondered whether it could possibly be the same Parisians who had also cheered Napoleon and then himself in such rapid succession?'(From Alistair Horne, The Age of Napoleon*). Within weeks, however, a savage Bourbon backlash against republican and Bonapartist elements was unleashed, which became known as the 'White Terror'. The Ancien Régime, supported by a privileged aristocracy and a reactionary Roman Catholic Church, was back: for the time being at least.*

And this was good news for the British, who, effectively barred from the Continent for twenty years (unless sporting a red jacket and carrying a musket), descended on Paris in droves – via the battlefield of Waterloo, for a spot of macabre trophy-hunting – in order to lord it over their erstwhile enemies. It was also an opportunity to gawp at the impressive array of monuments, bridges, and public buildings erected by the 'Corsican Ogre', who by October 1815, was safely incarcerated on a speck of rock in the South Atlantic.

Meanwhile, the veterans of his Waterloo campaign – the so-called Army of the Loire – faced prejudice, persecution, and poverty. Despite this, however, they still had their pride, and as the Allied Army of Occupation settled down to enjoy the delights of Paris, an epidemic of duelling broke out, as Frenchmen of various political persuasions sought to spill each others' blood and those of their foreign oppressors.

Duelling has its origins in the chivalric code of the Middle Ages, where personal combat was encouraged as a means of settling differences. From this tradition, the 'duel of honour' emerged in seventeenth century Italy and quickly spread to France and the then to the rest of Europe. According to James Kelly, in That Damn'd Thing Called Honour, *'Duelling cannot be comprehended independent of the code of honour which gave it its raison d'être.' In other words, gentlemen were expected to demand satisfaction in a duel if they felt their honour had been insulted, and any man who refused to claim this prerogative was deemed a coward and consequently suffered an unbearable loss of face. Thus, the point of duelling was not so much to inflict death or injury, as to assert one's status as a 'man of honour'.*

Nevertheless, duelling was illegal in Britain and in theory, a duellist might be tried in a court of law: but as 'men of honour' were generally members of the ruling elite, this rarely occurred. In fact, in the British Army, an officer could be cashiered on the grounds of cowardice if he refused to fight a duel. Meanwhile, in France, duelling was something of a mania, despite being frowned upon by Napoleon. Before 1789 only aristocrats had the right to issue a challenge, but once the revolutionary ideal of Egalité was established, Frenchmen of all social classes claimed the right to fight duels, and 'affairs of honour' became a national pastime. The favoured weapon of the French duellist was the blade, while the British gentleman preferred to fight with pistols. In either instance, a strict duelling etiquette was followed, and the whole procedure was overseen by the antagonists' supporters or 'seconds'.

It only remains to be added that some gentlemen – excessively devoted to the code of honour – became notorious as duellists: the so-called 'fire-eaters', of whom Gronow may be classed as one. Although he refrains from describing his own 'affairs of honour', Gronow was a notorious duellist, an acknowledged marksman, and an expert on duelling etiquette, serving as a 'second' in more than one rencontre.

Paris After The Peace

In 1815 and the following years there were gathered together in Paris all the flower of English society: men of fashion and distinction, beautiful matrons and their still lovelier daughters. A history of all that occurred in those days would afford amusing materials for the pen of the novelist and tickle agreeably the ears of scandal-loving people. I shall, however, content myself with recording some of my own souvenirs.

Lord Castlereagh was the pre-eminent star of the autumn of 1815, 'the observed of all observers.'[1] He was here, there, and everywhere.

---

1 According to *The Journal of Mrs Arbuthnot*, Robert Stewart, Viscount Castlereagh, 'was above six feet high and had a remarkably fine commanding figure, very dark eyes, rather a high nose and a mouth whose smile was sweeter than it is possible to describe ... His manners were perfect as those of a high-born polished gentleman.'

Indeed, the mass of business he had to transact was so immense and the fatigue he had to undergo so great, that he was compelled to spend several hours each day in a bath, his nights being generally passed without sleep. His bath was always taken at the Bains Chinois, at the corner of the Rue de la Michodière. He was there shampooed by the celebrated Fleury and recruited his exhausted faculties by dozing for an hour or two. His favourite promenade was the gallery of the Palais Royal. In his walks he was almost always alone and used to dress very simply, never wearing any orders or decorations. On the other hand, Lady Castlereagh astonished the French by the magnificence of her diamonds. At the balls and parties she used to be followed about by envious women, affecting to admire but looking daggers all the while. On one occasion I heard a French lady exclaim, 'England is renowned for beautiful women; but when they are ugly, *elles ne le sont pas à-demi.*'[2] But this remark was as false as it was ill-natured, for Lady Castlereagh was rather handsome than otherwise.

The magnificent saloons of the *noblesses* in the Faubourg St Germain and the gorgeous *hôtels* of the ambassadors and ministers of the Allied Powers were thronged with fair ladies of all nations. Madame Edmond de Périgord, who died lately as Duchesse de Sagan, was remarkable for her wit and beauty. She was all-powerful with her uncle, Prince Talleyrand, and was a sort of queen in the diplomatic world. The Vicomtesse de Noailles was the Lady Jersey of the world of fashion; and though her face was not pretty, she, by her graceful *tournure* or skilful *toilette,* and clever conversation, drew after her a host of admirers. I might also name the Princesse de Beauveau and her daughters, the Comtesse d'Audenarde (with her splendid figure), Madame de Vaudreuil (with her handsome face and beautiful hands), the handsome Madame de Gourieff, the two Countesses Potoska and though last, not least in my recollection, the lovely Princess Bagration, with her fair hair and delicately formed figure. The Princess never wore

---

2 'When they are ugly, they are not half ugly.'

anything but white India muslin, clinging to her form and revealing it in all its perfection.

Among the English beauties were Lady Conyngham and her daughter, Lady Elizabeth; Lady Oxford and her three daughters; Lady Sydney Smith and her two beautiful relatives, the Misses Rumbold – one of whom, when already in the 'sere and yellow leaf' of old maidism, married Baron Delmar, a rich banker, and puffed up with *parvenu* pride, ruled over Parisian society with a rod of iron.

The Duke of Devonshire, then young, graceful, and distinguished, was hunted down by mothers and daughters with an activity, zeal and perseverance – and, I am sorry to add, a vulgarity – which those only can conceive who have beheld the British huntress in full cry after a duke. It was amusing to see how the ambitious matrons watched every movement and how furious they became if any other girl was more favoured than their own daughters by the attention of the Monarch of the Peak. The young ladies, on their side, would not engage themselves with anyone until all hope of the duke asking them to dance was at an end. But as soon as he selected a partner, the same young ladies would go in search of those whom they had rejected and endeavour to get opposite or somewhere near him.

I remember seeing a serious quarrel between two great ladies, who were only prevented from coming to extremities by the timely intervention of our ambassadress, Lady Elizabeth Stuart. There were at this time many men of rank and fortune among our countrymen: Lords Surrey, Sunderland, Grosvenor, Clare, and Messrs Beaumont, Leigh, Monatague, Standish, etc. Some of these were particular in their attention to Lady Elizabeth Conyngham, but her mother, who was bent on securing a ducal coronet for her handsome daughter, discouraged all attempts that were made in less high quarters. Rumour had even then whispered that, owing to family secrets of a very peculiar nature, the Duke of Devonshire had entered into a solemn engagement never to marry, and though I have reason to believe that this was entirely false, it is certain that he lived and died a bachelor. Besides this, he was always considered by those who knew him well to be very unlikely to fall in love with anyone.[3]

About this time (but I may sometimes make a mistake in the exact date of my *souvenirs*) the Duke of Gloucester arrived in Paris. He made himself conspicuous in aiding the elopement of Mr (afterwards Sir Charles) Shakerly with Mademoiselle d'Avaray, daughter of the Duke d'Avaray, an intimate friend of Louis XVIII. The young lady was only seventeen years of age and very handsome. It was the only case I can remember of a young French lady running away from her father's house and the sensation created by such an extraordinary event was very great. The marriage – as runaway marriages usually are – was a very unhappy one, and the quarrels of the ill-matched couple were so violent that the police had to interfere. Unfortunately the fair lady having once eloped, thought she might try the same experiment a second time, and one cold winter's night she decamped from a ball at the Austrian ambassador's with a black-haired Spanish don, the Marquis d'Errara.

☙· The Salon Des Étrangers In Paris

When the Allies entered Paris after the battle of Waterloo, the English gentlemen sought, instinctively, something like a club. Paris, however, possessed nothing of the sort, but there was a much more dangerous establishment than the London clubs, namely, a rendezvous for confirmed gamblers.[4] The Salon des Étrangers was most gorgeously furnished,

---

3 William George Spencer Cavendish, sixth duke of Devonshire (1790–1858), never married, despite being Britain's most eligible bachelor – although according to the *Oxford Dictionary of National Biography*: 'As a youth he had planned to marry his cousin, Lady Caroline Ponsonby, and was devastated by her marriage to William Lamb, later Viscount Melbourne. In November 1827 he began an alliance with Eliza Warwick, about whom little else is known, which remained a well-kept secret throughout its ten-year duration.'

4 Arthur Bryant noted that gambling in Paris 'was a universal fixation … both sexes crowded night after night into airless rooms where no sound was heard but the crack of the croupier's stick and the rattling of money. It shocked English visitors even more than the pornographic prints on the hotel walls.'

provided with an excellent kitchen and wines, and was conducted by the celebrated Marquis de Livry, who received the guests and did the honours with a courtesy that made him famous throughout Europe. The Marquis presented an extraordinary likeness to the Prince Regent of England, who actually sent Lord Fife over to Paris to ascertain this momentous fact. The play that took place in these saloons was frequently of the most reckless character: large fortunes were often lost, the losers disappearing, never more to be heard of. Among the English *habitués* were the Hon. George T__, the late Henry Baring, Lord Thanet, Tom Sowerby, Cuthbert, Mr Steer, Henry Broadwood, and Bob Arnold.

The Hon. George T__, who used to arrive from London with a very considerable letter of credit expressly to try his luck at the Salons des Étrangers, at length contrived to lose his last shilling at *rouge-et-noir*.[5] When he had lost everything he possessed in the world, he got up and exclaimed in an excited manner, 'If I had Canova's *Venus and Adonis* from Alton Towers, my uncle's country seat, it should be placed on *rouge,* for black has won fourteen times running!'

The late Henry Baring was more fortunate at hazard[6] than his countryman but his love of gambling was the cause of his being excluded from the banking establishment. Colonel Sowerby, of the Guards, was one of the most inveterate players in Paris, and as is frequently the case with a fair player, a considerable loser. But perhaps the most incurable gamester amongst the English was Lord Thanet, whose income was not less than £50,000 a year, every farthing of which he lost at play.[7] Cuthbert dissipated the whole of his fortune in like manner. In fact, I do not remember any instance where those who spent their time in this den did not lose all they possessed.

---

5   This game has been defined as 'A game of chance; so called because of the red and black diamonds marked on the board. The dealer deals out to noir first till the sum of the pips exceeds thirty, then to rouge in the same manner. That packet which comes nearest to thirty-one is the winner of the stakes.'

6   A dice game commonly regarded as the ancestor of craps.

7   Sackville Tufton, ninth earl of Thanet (1769–1825) was an infamous gambler, and is known to have lost £120,000 at the Salon des Étrangers in one night.

The Marquis de L__ had a charming villa at Romainville, near Paris, to which, on Sundays, he invited not only those gentlemen who were the most prodigal patrons of his *salon,* but a number of ladies, who were dancers and singers conspicuous at the opera, forming a society of the strangest character, the male portion of which were bent on losing their money, whilst the ladies were determined to get rid of whatever virtue they might still have left. The dinners on these occasions were supplied by the chef of the Salon des Étrangers, and were such as few *renommés* [celebrities] of the kitchens of France could place upon the table.

Amongst the constant guests was Lord Fife, the intimate friend of George IV,[8] with Mademoiselle Noblet, a *danseuse,* who gave so much satisfaction to the *habitués* of the pit at the opera, both in Paris and London. His Lordship spent a fortune upon her: his presents in jewels, furniture, articles of dress, and money, exceeded £40,000. In return for all this generosity, Lord Fife asked nothing more than the lady's flattery and professed affection.

Amongst others who visited the Salon des Étrangers were Sir Francis Vincent, Gooch, Green, Ball Hughes, and many others whose names I no longer remember. Of foreigners, the most conspicuous were Blücher, General Ornano, father-in-law of Count Walewski, Pactot, and Clari, as well as most of the ambassadors at the Court of the Tuileries. As at Crockford's, a magnificent supper was provided every night for all who thought proper to avail themselves of it. The games principally played were *rouge-et-noir* and hazard: the former producing an immense profit, for not only were the whole of the expenses of this costly establishment defrayed by the winnings of the bank, but a very large sum was paid annually to the municipality of Paris. I recollect a young Irishman, Mr Gough, losing a large fortune at this *tapis vert.* After returning home about two a.m., he sat down and wrote a letter, giving reasons as to why he was about to commit suicide: these, it is needless to say, were simply gambling reverses. A pistol shot through the brain terminated his existence. Sir Francis Vincent – a

8   At this time still the Prince Regent.

man of old family and considerable fortune – was another victim of this French hell, who contrived to get rid of his magnificent property, and then disappeared from society.

In calling up my recollections of the Salons des Étrangers, some forty years since, I see before me the noble form and face of the Hungarian Count Hunyady, the chief gambler of the day, who created considerable sensation in his time. He became *très à la mode:* his horses, carriage, and house were considered perfect, while his good looks were the theme of universal admiration; there were ladies' cloaks *à la Huniade,* and the illustrious Borel, of the Rocher de Cancalle, named new dishes after the famous Hungarian. Hunyady's luck for a long time was prodigious – no bank could resist his attacks – and at one time he must have been a winner of nearly 2,000,000 francs. His manners were particularly calm and gentlemanlike. He sat apparently unmoved, with his right hand in the breast of his coat, whilst thousands depended upon the turning of a card or the hazard of a die. His valet, however, confided to some indiscreet friend that his nerves were not of such iron temper as he would have made people believe, and that the count bore in the morning the bloody marks of his nails, which he had pressed into his chest in the agony of an unsuccessful turn of fortune. The streets of Paris were at that time not very safe: consequently, the count was usually attended to his residence by two *gendarmes,* in order to prevent his being attacked by robbers. Hunyady was not wise enough (what gamblers are?) to leave Paris with his large winnings, but continued as usual to play day and night. A run of bad luck set in against him and he lost not only the whole of the money he had won, but a very large portion of his own fortune. He actually borrowed £50 of the well-known Tommy Garth – who was himself generally more in the borrowing than the lending line – to take him back to Hungary.

⇗• The Palais Royal

France has often been called the centre of European fashion and gaiety, and the Palais Royal, at the period to which I refer, might be called the very heart of French dissipation. It was a theatre in which all the great actors of fashion of all nations met to play their parts. On this spot were congregated daily an immense multitude, for no other purpose than to watch the busy comedy of real life that animated the corridors, gardens, and saloons of that vast building. Mingled together and moving about the area of this oblong-square block of buildings, might be seen, about seven p.m., a crowd of English, Russian, Prussian, Austrian, and other officers of the Allied armies, together with countless foreigners from all parts of the world. Here too, might have been seen the present King of Prussia with his father and brother, the late king; the dukes of Nassau, Baden, and a host of Continental princes, who entered familiarly into the amusements of ordinary mortals, dining *incog.* at the most renowned restaurants and flirting with painted female frailty.

A description of one of the houses of the Palais Royal will serve to portray the whole of this French pandemonium. On the ground floor is a jeweller's shop, where may be purchased diamonds, pearls, emeralds, and every description of female ornament, such as only can be possessed by those who have very large sums of money at their command. It was here that the successful gambler often deposited a portion of his winnings and took away some costly article of jewellery, which he presented to some female friend who had never appeared with him at the altar of marriage. Beside this shop was a staircase – generally very dirty – which communicated with the floors above. Immediately over the shop was a café, at the counter of which presided a lady – generally of more than ordinary female attractions – who was very much *décolletée,* and wore an amount of jewellery that would have made the eye of an Israelite twinkle with delight. And there *la crème de la crème* of male society used to meet, sip their ice and drink their cup of mocha, whilst holding long conversations – almost exclusively about gambling and women.

Men's thoughts in this region seemed to centre night and day upon the *tapis vert,* and at the entrance of this *salon* was that fatal chamber, over which might have been written the famous line of Dante: '*Voi che entrate lasciate ogni speranza.*'[9] The reader will at once understand that

9 'Abandon hope all ye who enter here.'

I am referring to the gambling-house, the so-called 'hell' of modern society. In one room was the *rouge-et-noir* table, which, from the hour of twelve in the morning was surrounded by men in every stage of the gambling malady. There was the young pigeon who, on losing his first feather had experienced an exciting sensation, which if followed by a bit of good luck, gave him a confidence that the parasites around him – in order to flatter his vanity – would call 'pluck'. There were others in a more advanced stage of the fever, who had long since lost the greater part of their incomes. These men had not got to the last stage of gambling despair but they were so far advanced on the road to perdition that their days were clouded by perpetual anxiety, which reproduced itself in their very dreams. The gambler who has thus far advanced in his career lives in an *inferno* of his own creation: the charms of society, the beauty of woman, the attractions of the fine arts, and even the enjoyment of a good dinner, are to him rather a source of irritation than delight. The confirmed gamester is doing nothing less than perpetually digging a grave for his own happiness.

The third and most numerous group of men round the *tapis vert* consisted of a class most of whom had already spent their fortunes, exhausted their wealth, and lost their position in society, by the fatal and demoralising thirst for gold which still fascinated them. They became the hawks of the gambling table, their quick and wild-glancing eyes were constantly looking out for suitable game during the day and leaving it where it might be bagged at night. Both at the *rouge-et-noir* table and *roulette* the same sort of company might be met with. These gambling-houses were the very fountain of immorality: they gathered together under the most seductive circumstances – the swindler and the swindled. There were tables for all classes: the workman might play with twenty *sous* or the gentleman with 10,000 francs. The law did not prevent any class from indulging in a vice that assisted to fill the coffers of the municipality of Paris.

The floor over the gambling-house was occupied by unmarried women. I will not attempt to picture some of the saddest evils of the society of large cities but I may add that these *Phrynes*[10] lived in a style of splendour which can only be accounted for by the fact of their participating in the easily earned gains of the gambling-house *régime*.

At that time the Palais Royal was externally the only well-lighted place in Paris. It was the rendezvous of all idlers who lay out their attractions for the public at large. These were to be seen at all hours in full dress, their bare necks ornamented with mock diamonds and pearls, and thus decked in all their finery, they paraded up and down, casting their eyes significantly on every side.

Some strange stories are told in connection with the gambling-houses of the Palais Royal. An officer of the Grenadier Guards came to Paris on leave of absence, took apartments here, and never left it until his time of absence had expired. On his arrival in London, one of his friends inquired whether this was true, to which he replied, 'Of course it is, for I found everything I wanted there, both for body and mind.'

Such was the state of the Palais Royal under Louis XVIII and Charles X. The Palais Royal of the present day is simply a tame and legitimately commercial mart, compared with that of olden times. Society has changed: the government no longer patronises such nests of immorality, and though vice may exist to the same extent, it assumes another garb and does not appear in the open streets, as at the period to which I have referred.

🐾· The Café Tortoni

About the commencement of the present century, Tortoni, the centre of pleasure, gallantry and entertainment, was opened by a Neapolitan who came to Paris to supply the Parisians with good ice. The founder of this celebrated café was by name Veloni, an Italian whose father lived with Napoleon from the period he invaded Italy, when First Consul, down to his fall. Young Veloni brought with him his friend Tortoni, an industrious and intelligent man. Veloni died of an affection of the lungs shortly after the café was opened and left the business to Tortoni, who, by dint of care,

---

10 A reference to the mistress of the Ancient Greek sculptor, Praxiteles.

The Duke of Wellington pictured in 1813.

Marshal Blücher, Wellington's ally at Waterloo.

Wellington and Blücher meet at La Belle Alliance at the end of the battle of Waterloo.

Some British commanders during the Napoleonic Wars: (from left to right) Sir Thomas Graham, Lord Hill, Sir Thomas Picton and Lord Uxbridge.

Allied monarchs meet in Hyde Park after the fall of Napoleon: (from left to right) the King of Prussia, the Prince Regent and the Emperor of Russia.

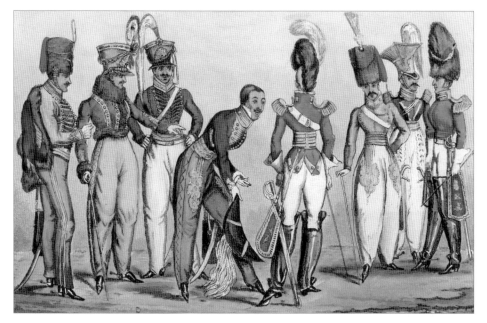

British uniforms in the period following the battle of Waterloo. This was a golden age for the military tailor.

British Life Guards on parade. These often acted as the Prince Regent's escort. Gronow chides them for their lack of energy during an attempt on the prince's life in 1819.

The occupation of Paris in 1815 was an international affair. Here British troops enjoy themselves around town.

The Russians also entered Paris. This unflattering sketch portrays the arrival of the Russian baggage train in the French capital.

Two nations eye each other warily. Paris was, according to Gronow, the 'centre of European fashion and gaiety' and the English took to it readily.

An English family, free to roam the Continent after years of warfare, 'sip their ice and drink their cup of mocha' in an elegant Parisian café.

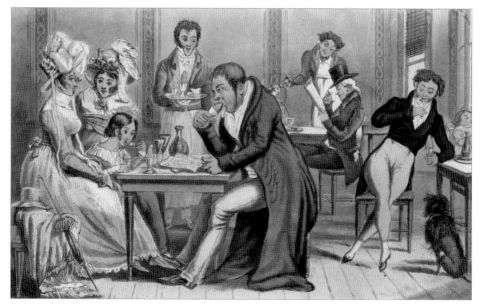

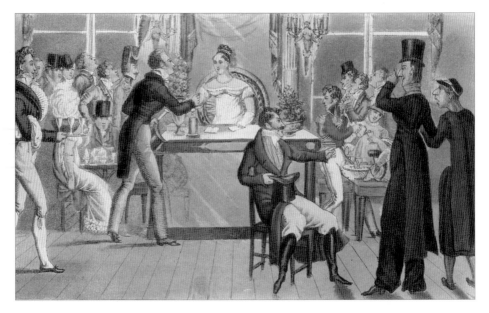

English visitors, both military and civilian, congregated at the Café des Milles Colonnes in Paris during the occupation.

Socialising at Parisian cafés and visiting the opera house allowed the occupiers to get to know the occupied.

A Quadrille being performed at Almack's assembly rooms, a venue which was notoriously difficult to access on account of its exclusive dress code.

An elegant ball being held at Almack's in 1815. Beau Brummel (second from the left) was a regular visitor.

Above: 'In those days the Minuet, Gavotte and Monaco were the favourite dances, and if a gentleman could muster sufficient grace and agililty, he was sure of receiving invitations.'

Below: More sobre work. A debate in the House of Commons. Gronow later took to politics.

Above: Fashionable London out driving or riding through Hyde Park.

Below: London's self-appointed dandies mustered in force at the numerous pleasure gardens throughout the capital.

The Prince Regent.

Maria Fitzherbert, the prince's 'wife'.

The interior of Carlton House, 'one of the most ugly edifices that ever disfigured London'.

Above: Regulars at White's Club in St James's Street: (left to right) Marquis of Londonderry, Colonel Cooke, Captain Gronow, Lord Allen and Count D'Orsay.

Below: Considerable fortunes were won and lost at Brooks's Club.

Beau Brummel's rise and fall transfixed
Regency London.

According to Gronow, Lady Jersey's bearing
was that of 'a theatrical tragedy queen'.

A grotesque sketch of London dandies ridiculing Sir Lumley Skeffington (left) and Lord Petersham (centre).

Then as now, one of London's most fashionable places to see and to be seen was the area around St James's Street.

Visitors to London opera houses included (from left to right) Prince Esterhazy, Lord Fife, Ball Hughes and Lord Wilton.

Prominent celebrities of London and Paris; Wellington (left, Talleyrand (centre) and the Count D'Orsay (right).

Gronow's aquaintances included such London figures as (left to right) Lord Westmoreland, Colonel Upton, Townshend and Tom Raikes.

Other Regency notables included Lord Alvanley (left), Lord Hill (centre) and Lord Yarmouth. Gronow considered Alvanley to be 'the wittiest man of his day'.

Gambling at Crockford's Club. Gronow notes, 'drinking and playing were more universally indulged in' and London had dozens of gambling dens.

Many of the gaming clubs were around St James's. Play was for such high stakes that 'ravages in large fortunes' were made. George Drummond once lost £20,000 to Brummel at whist.

economy, and perseverance, made his café renowned all over Europe. Towards the end of the First Empire and during the return of the Bourbons and Louis Philippe's reign, this establishment was so much in vogue that it was difficult to get an ice there: after the opera and theatres were over, the Boulevards were literally choked up by the carriages of the great people of the Court and the Faubourg St Germain bringing guests to Tortoni's.

The Duchess of Berri with her suite came nearly every night *incognito;* the most beautiful women Paris could boast of, old maids, dowagers, and old and young men, pouring out their sentimental twaddle and holding up to scorn their betters, congregated here. In fact, Tortoni's became a sort of club for fashionable people: the saloons were monopolised by them and became the rendezvous for all that was carefree – and I regret to add – immoral.

Gunter, the eldest son of the founder of the house in Berkley Square arrived in Paris about this period, to learn the art of making ice, for prior to the peace, our London ices and creams were acknowledged (by the English as well as foreigners) to be detestable. In the early part of the day, Tortoni's became the rendezvous of duellists and retired officers, who congregated in great numbers to breakfast, which consisted of cold *patés*, game, fowl, fish, eggs, broiled kidneys, iced champagne, and liqueurs from every part of the globe.

Though Tortoni succeeded in amassing a large fortune, he suddenly became morose and showed evident signs of insanity. In fact, he was the most unhappy man on earth. On going to bed one night, he said to the lady who superintended the management of his café, 'It is time for me to have done with the world.' The lady thought lightly of what he said, but upon quitting her apartment on the following morning, she was told by one of the waiters that Tortoni had hanged himself.

Among the prominent and singular personages who used daily to visit this café was the Russian Prince Tuffiakin, who was immensely rich and perhaps the greatest epicure in Paris. When he attained the respectable age of seventy, he fell desperately in love with a beautiful girl named Anna Sinclair, who was born of Scotch parents. Upon one occasion, whilst sipping his ice, the old man observed his adored Anna ogling a young dandy and a serious quarrel was the consequence: however, in course of time, a sort of truce was patched up between the lovers. The fair Scotch girl promised never more to ogle and the old man proposed the following plan of reconciliation: they were both to meet at the church of Notre Dame de Lorette and exchange rings at the altar, and afterwards to leave the church arm in arm. Though Tuffiakin was of a jealous disposition, he was nevertheless a great libertine, for he pretended to be in love with every pretty girl he met. He suddenly became enamoured of a well-known *danseuse,* who was living under the protection of an English nobleman. The prince, well knowing the power of his money, boldly presented himself at the lady's house and by the application of an immense bribe of money and jewels, he succeeded in obtaining the good graces of the inconstant daughter of Terpsichore. This old Russian *débauché* hastened his death by his excesses and became an idiot.

It was the custom for the great ladies who came to Tortoni's to form their parties there, and I recollect as if it had occurred yesterday, that upon one occasion the Princess Beauvau invited those who were assembled in the centre room, to meet at her hotel at midnight to dance. On our arrival, we were agreeably surprised to find Musard, Colinet, and other musicians assembled and ready to strike up a quadrille or a waltz. The charming daughters of the Princess, the Ladies Harley – with others whom I now forget – danced with all the grace of professional performers. In those days the Minuet, Gavotte, and Monaco were the favourite dances, and if a gentleman could muster sufficient grace and agility for any of those fashionable dances, he was sure of receiving invitations from the best houses in the Faubourg St Germain.

About the period I allude to, a young captain in one of the French regiments of hussars made his appearance at Tortoni's: the Count Walewski, a natural son of the great Napoleon's. He was remarkable for his good looks, the ladies adored him, and it must be acknowledged he was one of the finest-looking men I ever saw. Not liking a military life, Walewski retired from the hussars and adopted politics, in which sphere he soon evinced considerable talent. His friends the Ducs de Morny and Mouchy, the Counts Antonin and Louis Noailles, the Counts Montguyon and Lavallette, met here nearly every night. Upon one occasion, a strange scene took place between Lavallette and Montguyon, owing to a pretty girl, Mademoiselle D__, with whom it was said that they were both in love. Be this as it may, the Green Eyed-Monster was aroused and from high words, a duel was the consequence: they fought with swords and Montguyon received a wound in the arm, when the seconds interfered and put an end to the affair.

The Revolution of 1830[11] was a death-blow to Tortoni's. Persons in the best society, who had during many years been considered proud and exclusive, now began to keep entirely aloof and studiously avoided going there because of the new set that had been formed. This café, nevertheless, for some time continued to be in fashion and the rendezvous of persons of celebrity. Victor Hugo, Lamartine, Sophie Gay, Alexandre Dumas, the bankers Rothschild and the moneyed aristocracy, frequently met there. Clubs have, however, sprung up in Paris in every direction within a few years and the consequence has been that Tortoni's has lost its *renommée*. But nevertheless, the ices here are still considered the best in Paris.

≈· The Opera In Paris In 1815
The English flocked to the opera, and occupied some of the best boxes. The *corps de ballet* was at that time very efficient, and possessed some of the handsomest women and best dancers in Europe. This reminds me of an amusing incident. General D __, a fine old veteran of the empire, and an *habitué* of the *coulisses*[12] at the time I speak of, asked me a few years since to accompany him to the opera, which, from a prolonged absence from Paris, he had not visited for many years. When we arrived, after taking a good survey with his glass, he observed, 'I find they now call the young

---

11 The so-called 'July Revolution', which overthrew Charles X, the last of the Bourbons, and ushered in the reign of Louis-Philippe.
12 The backstage dressing-rooms in a theatre.

ladies we used to call *figurantes*[13] *des rats de opera*:[14] I am curious to see them again.' At this moment a whole army of young, more or less pretty, came fluttering across the stage. My friend looked at them attentively with his *lorgnette,* and at last exclaimed, with a sigh, 'Mais je ne reconnais plus ces rats là.'[15] 'Je crois bien, mon Général,' said I, 'les vôtres n'auraient plus de dents pour grignoter leur prochain.'[16]

Amongst the most remarkable dancers, were the inimitable Bigottini, Legros, Fanny Bias, Lacroix, Brocard, Noblet, Martin, Baron, and the short *trapue* [squat] Madame Montessu, with her large head, thick legs, and powerful *pointes.* It was a curious sight to behold ambassadors and great state functionaries assembled in the *foyer de danse,* paying court to the *danseuses.* The most conspicuous of these gentlemen were the dukes de la Rochefoucauld, de Gramont, Fitzjames, and Maille: all attired in knee-breeches and opera hats, and with buckles in their shoes and frills and ruffles of the costliest kind. After the opera, these same personages retired to the *Salon des Étrangers,* where they generally spent an hour or two collecting all the gossip they could hear, in order to divert the king. There was not a scandalous story that was not retailed by those gentlemen for their master's recreation.

Among our countrymen who had the *entrée* to the *foyer* or green room, Lord Fife made himself the most conspicuous by his unremitting attentions to Mlle Noblet, whom he never quitted for an instant. He would carry her shawl, hold her fan, run after her with her scent-bottle in his hand, admire the diamond necklace someone else had given her, or gaze in ecstasy on her pirouettes. On his return to London, the old *roué* would amuse George IV with a minute description of the lady's legs, and her skill in using them. Horses' legs are frequently the cause of the ruin of numbers of our aristocracy, but in the case of Lord Fife, the beautiful shape of the supporters of Mlle Noblet had such an effect upon the *perfervidum*

---

13 Extras or bit-players.

14 Literally 'opera rats'.

15 'But I do not recognize these rats anymore.'

16 'I believe, general, that yours no longer have teeth with which to nibble.'

ingenium Scoti,[17] that he from first to last spent nearly £80,000 on this fair daughter of Terpsichore.

Another original much talked of about this time was Sir John Burke, who married a Miss Ball Hughes. He was known by the name of 'The Delegate Dandy', from having been sent on a mission to the Pope from the Irish Catholics. He was a great frequenter of the *coulisses* and the gaming-houses, where he would be seen nightly, rushing about from room to room, chattering the vilest French with unblushing effrontery, or making such a disturbance as to draw down on his bead curses both loud and deep from the gamblers, which, however, he received with perfect equanimity and good humour.

⚘· Escape Of Lavalette From Prison

Few circumstances created a greater sensation than the escape of Lavalette from the Conciergerie, after he had been destined by the French government to give employment to the guillotine. The means by which the prisoner avoided his fate and disappointed his enemies produced a deep respect for the English character, and led the French to believe that, however much the governments of France and England might be disposed to foster feelings either of friendship or of enmity, individuals could entertain the deepest sense of regard for each other, and that a chivalrous feeling of honour would urge them on to the exercise of the noblest feelings of our nature. This incident likewise had a salutary influence in preventing acts of cruelty and of bloodshed, which were doubtless contemplated by those in power.

Lavalette bad been, under the imperial government, head of the Post Office, which place he filled on the return of the Bourbons, and when the Emperor Napoleon arrived from Elba, he continued still to be thus employed. Doubtless, on every occasion when opportunity presented itself, he did all in his power to serve his great master: to whom, indeed,

---

17 'The intense earnestness of the Scotsman', a reference to R. Buchanan's line from *The Ten Years' Conflict, Being the History of the Disruption of the Church of Scotland*, published in 1849.

he was allied by domestic ties, having married into the Beauharnais family. When Louis XVIII returned to Paris after the battle of Waterloo, Lavalette and the unfortunate Marshal Ney were singled out as traitors to the Bourbon cause, and tried, convicted, and sentenced to death.[18]

The 26th December was the day fixed for the execution of Lavalette, a man of high respectability and of great conections, whose only fault was fidelity to his chief. On the evening of the 21st, the Madame Lavalette, accompanied by her daughter and her governess, Madame Dutoit, a lady of seventy years of age, presented herself at the Conciergerie, to take a last farewell of her husband. She arrived at the prison in a sedan chair. On this very day the Procureur-Général had given an order that no one should be admitted without an order signed by himself: the *greffier* [clerk of the court] having, however, on previous occasions been accustomed to receive Madame Lavalette with the two ladies who now sought also to enter the cell, did not object to it, so these three ladies proposed to take coffee with Lavalette. The under-gaoler was sent to a neighbouring café to obtain it, and during his absence Lavalette exchanged dresses with his wife. He managed to pass undetected out of the prison, accompanied by his daughter, and entered the chair in which Madame Lavalette had arrived, which, owing to the management of a faithful valet, had been placed so that no observation could be made of the person entering it. The bearers found the chair somewhat heavier than usual, but were ignorant of the change that had taken place, and were glad to find, after proceeding a short distance, that the individual within preferred walking home, and giving up the sedan to the young lady. On the *greffier* entering the cell, he quickly discovered the ruse and gave the alarm: the under-gaoler was despatched to stop the chair but he was too late.

---

18 Antoine-Marie Chamans, comte de Lavalette (1768–1830) – had married Emilie de Beauharnais, daughter of François de Beauharnais, the Empress Josephine's brother-in-law. As Lavalette had assisted Napoleon's escape from Elba, and Ney had betrayed Louis XVIII's confidence and deserted to his former emperor, the Bourbons decided to make an example of these prominent public figures: an unjust and unpopular move, which became part of the 'White Terror'.

Lavalette had formed a friendship with a young Englishman of the name of Bruce, to whom he immediately had recourse, throwing himself upon his generosity and kind feeling for protection, which was unhesitatingly afforded. But as Bruce could do nothing alone, he consulted two English friends who had shown considerable sympathy for the fate of Marshal Ney – men of liberal principles and undoubted honour, and both of them officers in the British service: these were Captain Hutchinson and General Sir Robert Wilson.[19] To the latter was committed the most difficult task, that of conveying out of France the condemned prisoner, and for this achievement few men were better fitted than Sir Robert Wilson, a man of fertile imagination, ready courage, great assurance, and singular power of command over others; who spoke French well, and was intimately acquainted with the military habits of different nations.

Sir Robert Wilson's career was a singular one. He had commenced life an ardent enemy of Bonaparte, and it was upon his evidence, collected in Egypt and published to the world, that the great general was for a long time believed to have poisoned his wounded soldiers at Jaffa. Afterwards he was attached to the Allied sovereigns in their great campaign; but upon his arrival in Paris, his views of public affairs became suddenly changed: he threw off the yoke of preconceived opinions, became an ardent liberal, and so continued to the last hours of his life. The cause of this sudden change of opinion has never been thoroughly known, but certain it is that on every occasion he supported liberal opinions with a firmness and courage that astonished those who had known him in his earlier days.[20]

Sir Robert undertook, in the midst of great dangers and difficulties, to convey Lavalette out of France. Having dressed him in the uniform of an English officer, and obtained a passport under a feigned name, he took

---

19 John Hely-Hutchinson (1787–1851), the future third earl of Donoughmore, and Sir Robert Thomas Wilson (1777–1849).

20 Although lavished with honours by the Russian and Austrian governments, with whose armies he had served with distinction as a liaison officer, Wilson received little recognition from his own, which viewed him rather suspiciously as a political freelancer. Wellington famously dubbed him, 'a very slippery fellow'.

him in a cabriolet past the barriers as far as Compiègne, where a carriage was waiting for them. They passed through sundry examinations at the fortified towns but fortunately escaped: the great difficulty being that, owing to Lavallette's having been the director of the posts, his countenance was familiar to almost all the postmasters who supplied relays of horses. At Cambrai three hours were lost, from the gates being shut, and at Valenciennes they underwent three examinations, but eventually they got out of France.

The police, however, became acquainted with the fact that Lavalette had been concealed in the Rue de Helder for three days, at the apartments of Mr Bruce, and this enabled them to trace all the circumstances, showing that it was at the apartments of Hutchinson that Lavalette had changed his dress, and that he had remained there the night before he quitted Paris. The consequence was that Sir Robert Wilson, Bruce, and Hutchinson were tried for aiding the escape of a prisoner, and each of them was condemned to three months' imprisonment: the under-gaoler, who had evidently been well paid for services rendered, had two years' confinement allotted to him.[21]

I went to see Sir Robert Wilson during his stay in the Conciergerie – a punishment not very difficult to bear, but which marked him as a popular hero for his life. A circumstance, I remember, made a strong impression on me, proving that, however great may be the courage of a man in trying circumstances, a trifling incident might severely shake his nerves. I was accompanied by a favourite dog of the Countess of Oxford's, which, being unaware of the high character of Sir Robert, or dissatisfied with his physiognomy, or for some good canine reason, took a sudden antipathy to

---

21 Wilson and his accomplices seem to have been arrested on 13th January 1816, three days after they had successfully spirited Lavalette out of the country. The Duke of York, commander in chief of the British Army, was obliged to issue a statement expressing the Prince Regent's displeasure at their actions. Meanwhile, Lavalette made good his escape to Bavaria, where he was aided by Eugène de Beauharnais, Napoleon's stepson. He later returned to Paris, however, and to his poor wife, who had been incarcerated for facilitating her husband's escape, and whose mind had been turned by the ordeal. Lavalette was officially pardoned in 1822.

him, and inserted his teeth into a somewhat fleshy part, but without doing much injury. The effect, however, on the general was extraordinary: he was most earnest to have the dog killed. I, being certain that the animal was in no way diseased, avoided obeying his wishes, and fear that I thus lost the good graces of the worthy man.

☞ An English Dandy In Paris

During the days of Georges III and IV, a number of gentlemen, remarkable for their eccentricities of dress and manners, were the lions of the day both in London and Paris. For example, we had such men as Brummell, Pierrepoint, John Mills, Meyler, Bradshaw, and others, who seemed to think that the principal object of their existence ought to be that of obtaining notoriety by their dress. In addition to this class, we had a series of fops about town, who were yet more extravagant in their dress and manners.

I well remember Captain T__ in Paris after the war. He lived in a magnificent style, having taken no less than two different hotels, which naturally created a good deal of gossip in the fashionable world. His carriages and horses were English and considered the most perfect things of the day. But the most remarkable feature of his eccentricities was the captain's dress: he wore trousers capacious enough for a Turk; his coat – which he always designed himself – was remarkable for its wide, bagged sleeves, and an ingenious mode of making the collar a sort of receptacle for a voluminous quantity of shirt frill; indeed, the shirt collar appeared to descend from his ears all the way down his back, so that you might suppose he was looking out of a black chimney pot.

Nature had bestowed upon him handsome features and a profusion of hair, which he had curled and arranged in such an eccentric style that the snaky locks appeared to be always desiring to escape from his head, and were only detained on his cranium by a tight-fitting little hat, suitable for a boy about fourteen. He wore a pair of golden spurs with rowels of the circumference of a small dessert plate. Thus he strutted about the streets of Paris, inviting the smiles of those who knew him and the positive laughter of strangers to whom he was unknown. When Mike Fitzgerald met him for the first time at the end of the war, he said, 'Well, T__, I am happy to find you have won your spurs: made of doubloons, I suppose.'

Peace to his ashes! He died in the flower of his age, much regretted by a large circle of his friends, and his death was mourned by nearly all the best families of the Faubourg St Germain, with whom he had lived on the most intimate and friendly terms for a quarter of a century.

🐝· How To Get Invited To A Ball

Mr Williams Hope's large fortune enabled him to give the most splendid entertainments to the *beau monde* of Paris.[22] At his balls and parties all the notables of the city were to be seen and no expense was spared to make them the most sumptuous entertainments then given. It was his custom, when the invitations were issued, not to open any letters till the party was over, to save him the mortification of refusing those who had not been invited.

It happened that a certain Marquis, well-known in Paris, who had married the sister of a prince, was desirous of being present at one of these assemblies, and accordingly wrote, requesting the favour of an invitation for himself, his wife, and his wife's sister, the Princess de C__. Receiving no answer, the Marquis called upon Mr Hope, who received him with his usual courtesy. The Marquis began by expressing his surprise that his letter had remained unanswered, when Mr Hope assured him that he had not received the letter in question, explaining the custom before alluded to. This explanation, however, did not satisfy the Marquis, who observed that such a proceeding was, to say the least of it, extraordinary, as letters were generally written in expectation of their receiving an answer with the least possible delay, and he added: 'Mr Hope, by your conduct you have not only insulted me, my wife and sister-in-law, but several of my friends. I must therefore tell you that the first time I meet you in the Champs Elysée

---

22 This anecdote concerns William Williams Hope, a wealthy and eccentric member of the Hope banking dynasty, who spent most of his time in Paris. He owned a stupendous set of diamonds, which he reputedly wore himself, and is said to have kept a harem of eighteen ladies.

or the Bois de Boulogne, I will give orders to my coachman to drive against your carriage, which insult you will naturally resent.' Mr Hope replied, 'I am not of your opinion as to the necessity of having my carriage injured through the awkwardness or stupidity of your coachman, and to avoid all further altercation, I will have the honour to send you as many cards of invitation to my next ball as you may wish for yourself and your friends.'

The Marquis swallowed the bait, returned to his wife, overcame the objections as to the manner in which the *entrée* was obtained, and appeared with her and his sister-in-law on the appointed evening. They were received with due honours and when supper was announced, Mr Hope advanced towards the Princess and offering her his arm, conducted her to the place of honour at his right hand at the supper table. The rank of Marquis and his sister-in-law had probably more influence than his threat in procuring for him the invitation, as the vanity and ostentation of Mr Hope were no less remarkable than his meanness and eccentricity.

⤳· English Soldiers On The Boulevards

An order had been given to the managers of all the theatres in Paris to admit a certain number of soldiers of the Army of Occupation free of expense. It happened that a party of the Guards, composed of a sergeant and a few men, went to the Théâtre des Variétés on the Boulevards, where one of the pieces, *Les Anglais pour Rire*,[23] was admirably acted by Potier and Brunet. In this piece, Englishwomen were represented in a very ridiculous light by those accomplished performers. This gave great offence to our soldiers and the sergeant and his men determined to put a stop to the acting: accordingly they stormed the stage and laid violent hands upon the actors, eventually driving them off. The police were called in and foolishly wanted to take our men to prison, but they soon found to their cost that they had to deal with unmanageable opponents, for the whole posse of *gendarmes* were charged and driven out of the theatre. A crowd assembled on the Boulevards, which however, soon dispersed

---

23 'Laughing at the English.'

when it became known that English soldiers were determined, *coûte qu'il coûte*, to prevent their countrywomen from being ridiculed. It must be remembered that the only revenge the Parisians were able to take upon their conquerors was to ridicule them, and the English generally took it in good humour and laughed at the extravagant drollery of the burlesque.

The English soldiers generally walked about Paris in parties of a dozen and were quiet and well-behaved.[24] They usually gathered every day on the Boulevard du Temple, where Punch and Judy was performed to the great amusement of our brave comrades. It was also the custom at the same period for the discharged officers of the Army of the Loire[25] to congregate there, and I remember witnessing the following incident.

During the performance of Punch, a diminutive, hunchbacked man made himself very noisy and troublesome to those in front of him. Two officers, wearing the Cross of the Legion of Honour were much annoyed at this and requested the dwarf to keep quiet and to leave off annoying them. The diminutive gentleman replied by abusing them and calling them *sacrés Bonapartistes,* an epithet of a disagreeable kind at that period, for it was not safe to be known by that denomination. The taller of the two officers, not relishing the impertinence of the dwarf, took him off the ground, placed him upon his shoulders, and walked up to Monsieur Guignol, saying, 'Take back your Punchinello, he has lost himself!' Our soldiers, who witnessed this practical joke and well-deserved lesson, gave the French officer three cheers. This mark of sympathy from an enemy had its desired effect and we became on excellent terms with our former brave antagonists, whom the fortune of war had deprived of their rank and pay, and who were to be pitied under the species of ostracism to which they were condemned.

---

24 According to Arthur Bryant the soldiers of the British Army of Occupation, 'quartered themselves in uncomfortable barracks or tents, paid on the nail, and often through the nose, for what they consumed, and, after the first few days, only entered Paris on passes. The least injury to civilian property was mercilessly punished ... When French veterans muttered sacré boeftake under their breath, or trod on their toes, they looked the other way and even sometimes apologised.'

25 That force which had survived Waterloo and constituted Napoleon's last field army.

During the time the troops remained we had only one man found dead in the streets: it was said that he had been murdered but of that there was considerable doubt, for no signs of violence were found. This was strongly in contrast to what happened to the Prussian soldiers. It was asserted – and indeed proved beyond a doubt – that numbers of them were assassinated, and in some parts of France it was not unusual to find in the morning, in deep wells or cellars, several bodies of soldiers of that nation who had been killed during the night – so strong was the hatred borne against them by the French.

⤳• Conduct Of The Prussians In Paris

The French had behaved so ill at Berlin after the battle of Jena in 1806, that the Prussians had sworn to be revenged if ever they had the opportunity to visit upon France the cruelties, the extortion, insults, and hard usage their own capital suffered: and they kept their word.[26]

I once saw a regiment of Prussians march down the Rue St Honoré when a line of half a dozen hackney-coachmen were quietly endeavouring to make their way in a contrary direction. Suddenly some Prussian soldiers left their ranks and with the butt-end of their muskets knocked the poor coachmen off their seats. I naturally felt ashamed at what I had seen, and being in uniform, some Frenchmen came up to me and requested me to report what I had witnessed to the Duke of Wellington. Upon my telling them it would be of no avail, they one and all said the English ought to blush at having allies and friends capable of such wanton brutality.

One afternoon, when upwards of 100 Prussian officers entered the galleries of the Palais Royal, they visited all the shops in turn, insulting

---

26 After Prussia's humiliating defeats at the Battles of Jena-Auerstädt in 1806, Napoleon dismembered the kingdom and saddled its remaining population of some 4,500,000 souls with a war indemnity of 154,000,000 francs – although he later claimed to have milked Prussia of a full one billion francs! According to E. F. Henderson, in *Blücher and the Uprising of Prussia Against Napoleon*, 'The burden fell on one and all and the hardships endured, as may be imagined, gave nourishment to the ever-growing hatred of Napoleon.'

the women and striking the men, breaking the windows and turning everything upside down: nothing, indeed, could have been more outrageous than their conduct. When information was brought to Lord James Hay of what was going on, he went out and arrived just as a troop of French *gendarmes* were on the point of charging the Prussians, then in the garden. He lost no time in calling out his men and placing himself between the *gendarmes* and the officers, said he should fire upon the first who moved. The Prussians then came up to him and said, 'We had all vowed to return upon the heads of the French in Paris the insults that they had heaped upon our countrymen in Berlin: we have kept our vow and we will now retire.' Nothing could equal the bitter hatred which existed – and still exists – between the French and the Prussians.

⚞· Marshal Blücher

Marshal Blücher, though a very fine fellow, was a rough diamond with the manners of a common soldier. On his arrival in Paris, he went every day to the *salon* and played the highest stakes at *rouge-et-noir*. The *salon*, during the time that the marshal remained in Paris, was crowded by persons who came to see him play. His manner of playing was anything but gentlemanlike and when he lost, he used to swear in German at everything that was French, looking daggers at the croupiers. He generally managed to lose all he had about him, also all the money his servant, who was waiting in the antechamber, carried. I recollect looking attentively at the manner in which he played: he would put his right hand into his pocket and bring out several *rouleaux* of *napoleons,* throwing them on the red or the black. If he won the first *coup,* he would allow it to remain, but when the croupier stated that the table was not responsible for more than 10,000 francs, then Blücher would roar like a lion and rap out oaths in his native language, which would doubtless have met with great success at Billingsgate if duly translated: fortunately, they were not heeded, as they were not understood by the lookers-on.

At that period there were rumours – and reliable ones too – that Blücher and the Duke of Wellington were at loggerheads. The Prussians wanted to blow up the Bridge of Jena, but the duke sent a battalion of our regiment to prevent it, and the Prussian engineers who were mining the bridge were civilly sent away: this circumstance created some ill-will between the chiefs.[27]

A sort of congress of the emperors of Austria and Russia and the King of Prussia (with Blücher and Wellington) met at the Hotel of Foreign Affairs, on the Boulevard, when, after much ado, the Duke of Wellington emphatically declared that if any of the monuments were destroyed he would take the British Army from Paris: this threat had the desired effect. Nevertheless, Blücher levied contributions on the poor Parisians and his army was newly clothed. The Bank of France was called upon to furnish him with several thousand pounds, which, it was said, were to reimburse him for the money lost at play. This, with many other instances of extortion and tyranny, was the cause of Blücher's removal, and he took his departure by order of the king.[28]

⇨• Duelling In France

When the restoration of the Bourbons took place, a variety of circumstances combined to render duelling so common that scarcely a day passed without one at least of these hostile meetings. Amongst the French themselves there were two parties always ready to distribute to each other *des coups d'épée*: the officers of Napoleon's army and the Bourbonist officers of

---

27 Wellington, quoted in Stanhope's *Conversations with Wellington*, is supposed to have commented 'About blowing up the bridge of Jena, there were two parties in the Prussian Army, Gneisenau and Müffling against, but Blücher violently for it. In spite of all I could do, he did make the attempt, even while I believe my sentinel was standing at one end of the bridge. But the Prussians had no experience in blowing up bridges. We, who had blown up so many in Spain could have done it in five minutes. The Prussians made a hole in one of the pillars, but their powder blew out instead of up, and I believe hurt some of their own people.'

28 As soon as Louis XVIII and his ministers arrived in Paris, 'Blücher's brief orgy of authority was over,' and when his somewhat draconian measures against the city and its population were consequently revoked, he handed in his resignation, declaring: 'I cannot and will not remain here any longer.'

the *Gardes du Corps.* Then again, there was the irritating presence of the English, Russian, Prussian, and Austrian officers in the French capital. In the duels between these soldiers and the French, the latter were always the aggressors.

At Tortoni's, on the Boulevards, there was a room set apart for such quarrelsome gentlemen where, after these meetings, they indulged in riotous champagne breakfasts. At this café might be seen all the most notorious duellists, amongst whom I can call to mind an Irishman in the *Gardes du Corps,* W__, who was a most formidable fire-eater. The number of duels in which he had been engaged would seem incredible in the present day: he is said to have killed nine of his opponents in one year.

The Marquis de H__, descended of an ancient family in Brittany, also in the *Gardes du Corps,* likewise fought innumerable duels, killing many of his antagonists. I have heard that on entering the army he was not of a quarrelsome disposition, but being laughed at and bullied into fighting by his brother officers, he, from the day of his first duel, like a wild beast that had once smelt blood, took a delight in such fatal scenes, and was ever ready to rush at and quarrel with anyone. The Marquis has now – I am glad to say – subsided into a very quiet, placable, and peace-making old gentleman: but at the time I speak of, he was much blamed for his duel with F__, a young man of nineteen. While dining at a café he exclaimed, *'J'ai envie de tuer quelqu'un!'*[29] and rushed out into the street and to the theatres, trying to pick a quarrel. But he was so well known that no one was found willing to encounter him. At last, at the Théâtre de la Porte St Martin, he grossly insulted this young man who was, I think, an *élève* of the École Polytechnique, and a duel took place under the lamp post near the theatre with swords. He ran F__ through the body and left him dead upon the ground.

The late Marshal St A__ and General J__ were great duellists at this time, with a whole host of others whose names I forget. The meetings generally took place in the Bois de Boulogne and the favourite weapon of

---

29 'I feel like killing somebody!'

the French was the small sword or the sabre; but foreigners, in fighting with the French (who were generally capital swordsmen) availed themselves of the use of pistols. The ground for a duel with pistols was marked out by indicating two spots which were twenty-five paces apart. The seconds then generally proceeded to toss up who should have the first shot: the principals were then placed and the word was given to fire.

The Café Foy, in the Palais Royal, was the principal place of rendezvous for the Prussian officers, and to this café the French officers on half-pay frequently proceeded in order to pick quarrels with their foreign invaders. Swords were quickly drawn and frequently the most bloody frays took place. These originated not in any personal hatred but from national jealousy on the part of the French, who could not bear the sight of foreign soldiers in their capital, which, when ruled by the great captain of the age had, like Rome, influenced the rest of the world. On one occasion our Guards, who were on duty at the Palais Royal, were called out to put an end to one of these encounters, in which fourteen Prussians and ten Frenchmen were either killed or wounded.

The French took every opportunity of insulting the English and very frequently, I am sorry to say, those insults were not met in a manner to do honour to our character. Our countrymen in general were very pacific, but the most awkward customer the French ever came across was my fellow-countryman, the late gallant Colonel Sir Charles S__, of the Engineers, who was ready for them with anything: sword, pistol, sabre, or fists – he was good at all – and though never seeking a quarrel, he would not put up with the slightest insult. He killed three Frenchmen in Paris in quarrels forced upon him. I remember in October 1815, being asked by a friend to dine at Beauvillier's, in the Rue Richelieu, when Sir Charles S__, who was well known to us, occupied a table at the farther end of the room. About the middle of the dinner we heard a most extraordinary noise and on looking up perceived that it arose from Sir Charles' table: he was engaged in beating the head of a smartly dressed gentleman with one of the long French loaves so well known to all who have visited France. On being asked the reason of such rough treatment, he said he would serve all Frenchmen in the same manner if they insulted him. The offence, it seems, proceeded from the person who had just been chastised in so summary a manner, and who had stared and laughed at Sir Charles in a rude way, for having ordered three bottles of wine to be placed upon his table. The upshot of this was a duel, which took place next day at a place near Vincennes and in which Sir Charles shot the unfortunate jester.

When Sir Charles returned to Valenciennes, where he commanded the Engineers, he found on his arrival a French officer waiting to avenge the death of his relation, who had only been shot ten days before at Vincennes. They accordingly fought before Sir Charles had time even to shave himself or eat his breakfast, he having only just arrived in his *coupé* from Paris. The meeting took place in the fosse of the fortress and the first shot from Sir Charles' pistol killed the French officer, who had actually travelled in the diligence from Paris for the purpose – as he boasted to his fellow-travellers – of killing an Englishman.

I recollect dining in 1816 at Hervey Aston's, at the Hôtel Breteuil in the Rue de Rivoli, opposite the Tuileries, where I met Seymour Bathurst and Captain E__ of the Artillery, a very good-looking man. After dinner, Mrs Aston took us as far as Tortoni's, on her way to the Opera. On entering the café, Captain E__ did not touch his hat according to the custom of the country but behaved himself *à la* John Bull, in a noisy, swaggering manner: upon which General (then Colonel) J__ went up to E__ and knocked off his hat, telling him that he hoped he would in future behave himself better. Aston, Bathurst, and I waited for some time, expecting to see E__ knock J__ down or at all events, give him his card as a preliminary to a hostile meeting on receiving such an insult: but he did nothing.

We were very much disgusted and annoyed at a countryman's behaving in such a manner and after a meeting at my lodgings, we recommended Captain E__, in the strongest terms, to call out Colonel J__, but he positively refused to do so, as he said it was against his principles. This specimen of the white feather astonished us beyond all measure. Captain E__ shortly after received orders to start for India, where I believe he died of cholera: in all probability of *funk*.

I do not think that Colonel J__ would altogether have escaped with impunity such a gratuitous insult to an English officer, but he retired into the country almost immediately after the incident at Tortoni's and could not be found.

There were many men in our army who did not thus disgrace the British uniform when insulted by the French. I cannot omit the names of my old friends, Captain Burges, Mike Fitzgerald, Charles Hesse, and Thoroton: each of whom, by their willingness to resent gratuitous offences, showed that insults to Englishmen were not to be committed without impunity. The last-named officer having been grossly insulted by Marshal V__, without giving him the slightest provocation, knocked him down: this circumstance caused a great sensation in Paris and brought about a court of inquiry, which ended in the acquittal of Captain Thoroton.

My friend, B__, though he had only one leg, was a good swordsman and contrived to kill a man at Lyons who had jeered him about the loss of his limb at Waterloo. My old esteemed friend, Mike Fitzgerald, son of Lord Edward and the celebrated Pamela, was always ready to measure swords with the Frenchmen, and after a brawl at Silvé's, the then fashionable Bonapartist café at the corner of the Rue Lafitte and the Boulevard, in which two of our Scotch countrymen showed the white feather, he and another officer placed their own cards over the chimneypiece in the principal room of the café, offering to fight any man – or number of men – for the frequent public insults offered to Britons. This challenge, however, was never answered.

A curious duel took place at Beauvais during the occupation of France by our army. A Captain B__, of one of our cavalry regiments quartered in that town, was insulted by a French officer. B__ demanded satisfaction, which was accepted, but the Frenchman would not fight with pistols and B__ would not fight with swords: so at last it was agreed that they should fight on horseback with lances. The duel took place in the neighbourhood of Beauvais and a crowd assembled to witness it. B__ received three wounds, but by a lucky prod, eventually killed his man. My late friend the Baron de P__, so well-known in Parisian circles, was second to the Frenchman on this occasion.

A friend of mine, certainly not of a quarrelsome turn but considered by his friends, on the contrary, as rather a good-natured man, had three duels forced upon him in the course of a few weeks. He had formed a *liaison* with a person whose extraordinary beauty got him into several scrapes and disputes. In January 1817, a few days after this acquaintance had been formed, Jack B__, well-known at that time in the best society in London, became madly in love with the fair lady and attempted one night to enter her private box at Drury Lane. This my friend endeavoured to prevent: violent language was used and a duel was the consequence. The parties met a few miles from London, in a field close to the Uxbridge Road, where B__, who was a hot-tempered man, did his best to kill my friend, but after the exchange of shots they were parted by their seconds. B__ was the son of Lady Bridget B__ and the seconds were Payne, uncle to George Payne, and Colonel Joddrell of the Guards.

Soon after this incident, my friend accompanied the lady to Paris, where they took up their residence at Meurice's in the Rue de l'Echiquier. The day after their arrival, they went out to take a walk in the Palais Royal and were followed by a half-pay officer of Napoleon's army, Colonel D__, a notorious duellist, who observed to the people about him that he was going to bully '*un Anglais*'. This man was exceedingly rude in his remarks – uttered in a loud voice – and after every sort of insult expressed in words, he had the impudence to put his arm round the lady's waist. My friend indignantly asked the colonel what he meant: upon which the ruffian spat in my friend's face. But he did not get off with impunity, for my friend, who had a crab stick in his hand, caught him a blow on the side of the head that dropped him. The Frenchman jumped up and rushed at the Englishman, but they were separated by the bystanders. Cards were exchanged and a meeting was arranged to take place the next morning in the neighbourhood of Passy.

When my friend, accompanied by his second, Captain H__ of the 18th, came upon the ground, he found the colonel boasting of the number of officers of all nations whom he had killed and saying, 'I'll now complete my list by killing an Englishman: *Mon petit, tu auras bientôt ton compte, car je tire fort bien.*[30] My friend quietly said, '*Je ne tire pas mal non plus,*'[31] and the duel took place. The colonel, who seems to have been a horrible ruffian, after a good deal more swaggering and bravado, placed himself opposite and on the signal being given, the colonel's ball went through my friend's whiskers, whilst his ball pierced his adversary's heart, who fell dead without a groan.

This duel made much noise in Paris and the survivor left immediately for Chantilly, where he passed some time. On his return to Paris, the second of the man who had been killed, Commander P__, insulted and challenged my friend. A meeting was accordingly agreed upon and pistols were again the weapons used. Again my friend won the toss and told his second, Captain H__, that he would not kill his antagonist – though he richly deserved death for wishing to take the life of a person who had never offended him – but that he would give him a lesson which he should remember. My friend accordingly shot his antagonist in the knee, and I remember to have seen him limping about the streets of Paris twenty years after this event.

When the result of this duel was known, not less than eleven challenges from Bonapartists were received by the gentleman in question, but any further encounters were put a stop to by the Minister of War or the Duc d'Angoulême – I forget which – who threatened to place the officers under arrest if they followed up this quarrel any further. When the news reached England, the Duke of York said that my friend could not have acted otherwise than he had done in the first duel, considering the gross provocation that he had received, but he thought it would have been better if the second duel had been avoided.

In the deeds I have narrated, the English seem to have had the advantage, but many others were killed or wounded. These I have not mentioned, as their details do not recur to my memory: but I do not remember an occasion on which Frenchmen were not the aggressors.

---

30 'My boy, you will soon receive your due, as I shoot extremely well.'
31 'I do not shoot badly either.'

At a somewhat later period than this, the present Marquis H__, then Lord B__, had a duel with the son of the Bonapartist General L__. General S__ was Lord B__'s second and the principals exchanged several shots without injury to either party. This duel, like the preceding, originated with the Frenchman, who insulted the Englishman at the Théâtre Français in the most unprovoked manner. At the present day our fiery neighbours are much more amenable to reason and if you are but civil, they will be civil to you – duels consequently are of rare occurrence. Let us hope that the frequency of these hostile meetings and the *animus* displayed in them originated in national wounded vanity rather than in personal animosity.

⚑· Englishmen In Paris

In the year 1817 Lord A__, his brother, and another friend, were staying in Paris. They had dined one day at Véry's – then the famous restaurant in the Palais Royal – and the conversation turned upon the insults offered by the Parisians, particularly the military, to the English visitors. His Lordship was silent during this conversation but took note of what had been said, while imbibing some potent Burgundy, and his imagination was none the weaker for having thus 'bottled it up'. On leaving the restaurant the first thing he did was to kick over a basket of toothpicks, which were presented to him for purchase, the next was to shove off the pavement a Frenchman, who proved to be an officer. Of course, there was a violent altercation: cards were exchanged and each party went his way to make arrangements for the 'pistols and coffee for four'.

Our countrymen, when near home, picked up their friend Manners – who had been shut out of his lodgings – and promised to accommodate him with a sofa at their rooms. On their arrival, he partially uncased and wrapped himself up in a large Witney blanket and greatcoat and then turned in. At an early hour the next morning, two gentlemen called on our countrymen and were ushered into the saloon. The first who presented himself to receive them was his Lordship, who had nothing on but a large pair of trousers and a cotton nightcap full of holes: he being so particular about having it aired that it was constantly singed in the process. Not speaking French, he requested his servant to act as interpreter and asked the strangers the object of their visit – the incidents of the preceding night having passed off from his memory with the fumes of the Chambertin. The discussion that ensued woke up Manners, who, wrapped in his blanket, rose from his couch, looking more like a white bear than anything else. It also drew from his dormitory Captain Meade, who made his appearance from a side door, clothed only in his nightshirt and a pair of expansive Russia duck trousers, whistling – as was his wont – and spitting occasionally through a hole that had been bored in one of his front teeth, in imitation of the stagecoachmen of the day. Lord A__'s brother next appeared on the scene in a costume little more complete than those of the others.

The visitors, although astonished at the appearance of the group, proceeded to business. Manners conducted it on the part of his friends, who could not speak French, and with a view of discharging his office more comfortably, drew aside the folds of his Witney blanket and placed his back against the mantelpiece, to enjoy the warmth of the glowing wood-ashes in the grate below. The Frenchmen were refused an apology by our friends, coupled with the observation that, with Englishmen, the case would be different, but that it was impossible on the present occasion to arrange matters in that way. They therefore requested the other party to name their weapons. Manners coolly informed them that they had decided on using *fusils* at twelve paces! This seemed rather to astonish the Frenchmen: they exchanged glances and then cast their eyes round the room and on the strange figures before them. Meade was whistling through his teeth, Lord A__, whose coppers were rather hot, had thrust his head out into the street through a pane of glass that had been smashed the night before, while the others were stalking about the room in their rather airy costumes. The gravity of the Frenchmen was overcome by the ludicrous aspect and *sang froid* of their opponents and they burst out laughing. Lord A__, who was as full of fun as he was of pluck, stretching out his hand to the injured party said, 'Come, I see you are good fellows, so shake hands. I had taken rather too much wine last night.' I need not say that the proffered hand was accepted and the French officers retired. After their departure, Manners asked the servant what *fusil* really meant, as when naming the weapon to be used, he supposed it to be a kind of pistol.

🦎· A Fire-Eater Cowed

A singular incident occurred at the Café Français in 1816. A celebrated duellist entered and began insulting all the persons who were seated at dinner. He boasted of his courage and declared his determination to kill Monsieur de F__. A gentleman present, disgusted at such braggart insolence, quietly walked up to this fire-eater and addressed him thus: 'As you are such a dangerous customer, perhaps you will accommodate me by being punctual at the entrance of the Bois de Boulogne, near the Porte Maillot, at midday tomorrow: earlier I cannot get there, but depend upon my arriving in due time with swords and pistols.' The duellist began to demur, saying he did not know what right a stranger had to take up the cudgels of M. de F__, to which the gentleman replied: 'I have done so because I am anxious to rid society of a dangerous fellow like yourself and would recommend you, before you go to your bed, to make your will. I will undertake to order your coffin and pay your funeral expenses.' He then gave the waiter a note of 1,000 francs with the injunction that his orders should be executed before eleven the following day. This had the desired effect of intimidating the bully, who left Paris the following day and never more was heard of or seen in public.

🦎· An Insult Rightly Redressed

Soon after the restoration of the Bourbons, several duels took place for the most frivolous causes. Duels were fought in the daytime and even by night. The officers of the Swiss Guards were constantly measuring swords with the officers of the old *Garde Impériale.* Upon one occasion a Frenchman, determined to insult a Swiss officer who, in the uniform of his regiment, was quietly taking his ice at Tortoni's, addressed him thus: 'I would not serve my country for the sake of money, as you do. We Frenchmen think only of honour.' To which the other promptly retorted, 'You are right, for we both of us serve for what we do not possess.' A duel was the consequence. They fought with swords under a lamp in the Rue Taitbout and the Frenchman was run through the body. But luckily the wound, though dangerous, did not prove fatal.

♠· A Duel Between Two Old Friends

General A. de Girardin, some forty years back, had a serious quarrel with one of his old friends, the Marquis de Briancourt, about a lady. A duel was the consequence. Pistols were chosen, but prior to exchanging shots de Girardin's second went – as was the custom – and felt the right side of his friend's antagonist but found nothing there to indicate the existence of padding. Accordingly, after measurement of the ground, pistols were handed to the combatants. The Marquis changed his pistol from his right to his left hand, both parties fired, and the Marquis fell. The seconds flew to the aid of the wounded man, but to their astonishment, on opening his waistcoat, several sheets of thick paper were found folded over the region of the heart. Notwithstanding this device, the blow from the bullet created a sore on the left side, which was never effectually cured. The Marquis died shortly afterwards.

♠· Fayot, Champion Of The Legitimists

Fayot fought more duels than any man in France. His aim with a pistol was certain, but he was not cruel and he usually wounded his adversary either in the leg or arm. He was likewise a good swordsman. General Fournier[32] was afraid of Fayot and only once measured swords with him, while the latter had a horror of Fournier for having killed so many young men belonging to good families. In his *rencontre* with Fayot, the general was severely wounded in the hand and ever after Fayot hunted his antagonist from one end of France to the other, determined to put an end to the 'Assassin' as he was called: but the Revolution came and all was chaos.

---

32 General François Fournier-Sarlovèze (1773–1827). John R. Elting, in *Swords Around A Throne*, called Fournier a psychopath who, 'took a sadistic pleasure in forcing duels on civilians (sometimes by insulting their wives) and then killing them leisurely, but always within the forms of the duelling code.'

Fayot's father was guillotined in the south of France in 1793. His mother, after the severe loss she had sustained in the death of her husband, whom she adored, brought up her son at Avignon, telling him, as he grew up to be a man, to take every opportunity of avenging the death of his father. Upon the restoration of the Bourbons, Fayot came to Paris where, by his singular manners and dress, he laid himself open to remark and ridicule. In the daytime he was usually dressed in a green coat, white waistcoat and neckcloth, leather pantaloons and Hessian boots, with his hat on one side. He visited London in 1814, where he bought a tilbury and horse, which he brought to Paris, and in this gig he paraded every day up and down the Boulevards, from the Rue Lafitte to the Place de la Madeleine. His evenings were generally passed either at Tortoni's or Silvé's, the respective rendezvous of the Bonapartists and Bourbons. In one or other of these cafés Fayot was sure to be found. He publicly gave out that he was ready to measure swords with anyone who dared to insinuate anything against the royal family: a threat sure to bring upon him serious *rencontres:* but nothing intimidated him. It was reported at the time – and generally believed – that he had, in the short period of two years, fought thirty duels without having been seriously wounded.

Upon one occasion Fayot repaired to the Théâtre Français to see *Germanicus.* Party spirit ran high and any allusion complimentary to the fallen emperor was received by the Bonapartists with applause. Fayot loudly hissed, and a great uproar arose when Fayot entered the breach by proclaiming himself the champion of Legitimacy. The consequence was that cards flew about the pit. Fayot carefully picked them up and placed them in his hat. After the play had terminated he repaired to Tortoni's, where he wrote his address upon several pieces of paper, which he distributed all over the Boulevards, stating that he was to be found every morning between the hours of eleven and twelve at the well in the Bois de Boulogne, near Auteuil.

Strange to say, after all this row at the theatre only one antagonist was forthcoming. On the second day, at the hour appointed, a gentleman arrived with his seconds, who found Fayot in his tilbury, ready for the fight. The name of his antagonist was a Monsieur Harispe, son of the distinguished Basque general.[33] Pistols were chosen and at the first discharge Fayot shot his adversary in the knee. Then, taking off his hat, he left the ground and proceeded to Paris in his tilbury to breakfast at Tortoni's, where a great many persons had congregated to know the result of this terrible duel.

The Revolution of 1830 drove Fayot away from Paris and he retired to his native Avignon, where he lived much respected by the principal inhabitants of that quaint town. In passing through Avignon some twelve years back, I called upon him and found him much altered, but still dressed in his original costume: the green coat, white neckcloth, etc.

ᔰ· Pistol-Shooting

One evening, in the Salon des Étrangers, I was introduced to General F__, a very great duellist[34] and the terror of every regiment he commanded: he was considered by Napoleon to be one of his best cavalry officers but was never in favour in consequence of his duelling propensities. It was currently reported that F__, in a duel with a very young officer, lost the toss and his antagonist fired first at him, when, finding he had not been touched, he deliberately walked close up to the young man, saying, '*Je plains ta mère*,'[35] and shot him dead. But there were some doubts of the truth of this story and I trust, for the honour of humanity, that it was either an invention or a gross exaggeration.

The night I was introduced to F__, I was told to be on my guard, as he was a dangerous character. He was very fond of practising with pistols and I frequently met him at Lapage's, the only place at that time where gentlemen used to shoot. F__, in the year 1822, was very corpulent and wore an enormous cravat, in order, it was said, to hide two scars received in battle. He was a very slow shot.

---

33 General, later Marshal, Jean-Isadore Harispe (1768–1855),a veteran of the war in Spain.

34 The afore-mentioned Fournier, who was known as the 'Demon of the Grand Army'.

35 'I grieve for your mother'.

The famous Junot, Governor-General of Paris, whom I never saw, was considered to be the best shot in France. My quick shooting surprised the *habitués* at Lapage's, where we fired at a spot chalked on the figure of a Cossack painted on a board and by word of command, 'One, two, three!' F__, upon my firing and hitting the mark forty times in succession, at the distance of twenty paces, shrieked out, *'Tonnerre de dieu, c'est magnifique!'* We were ever afterwards on good terms and supped frequently together at the *Salon*. At Manton's, on one occasion, I hit the wafer nineteen times out of twenty. When my battalion was on duty at the Tower in 1819, it happened to be very cold and much snow covered the parade and trees. For our amusement it was proposed to shoot at the sparrows in the trees from Lady Jane Grey's room, and it fell to my lot to bag eleven without missing one. This, I may say without flattering myself, was considered the best pistol-shooting ever heard of.

The Gardes Du Corps

I knew several of those gentlemen who had succeeded in getting into the companies of the *Gardes du Corps:* St Arnaud, Fouquainville, Odoard, Warrelles, St Roman, Fromasson, and though last, not least, Warren – an Irishman by birth, but whose father had married a French lady. Warren stood six feet four inches in height and was an extremely powerful man. He was always in hot water with his comrades and had fought duels with several of them, and his face and body showed marks of sabre cuts. Indeed, fighting and drinking were his delights. I never saw a man so violent, and when he had finished his bottle of champagne (and a few glasses of brandy) he became quite outrageous. He usually breakfasted, when off duty, at Tortoni's, upon beefsteaks and broiled kidneys, and anyone to whom he bore a grudge who entered the room at that moment was sure to be roughly handled.

It happened that Monsieur __, a distinguished painter, had returned to Paris from England, where he had played a shameful and disgusting part. The painter had been employed by the celebrated Mr Hope[36] of

---

36 Thomas Hope (1769–1831), from the same family of financiers as William Williams Hope, mentioned above, was a noted scholar, writer, and patron of the Arts.

Duchess Street to paint the portrait of his wife, Mrs Hope, afterwards lady Beresford. When the painting was finished, Mr Hope objected to pay for it, stating that it was a daub. The enraged painter, determined to be revenged, took the portrait home with him and in a few days returned it with the addition of a beast representing Mr Hope in the presence of his beautiful wife. A trial was the consequence and the painter was cast in damages. After this untoward event, London proved too hot for the Frenchman and he returned to Paris, where his imprudence in speaking in no measured terms of the English got him into a scrape that cost him his life.

The painter (unluckily for him) arrived at Tortoni's to breakfast at the moment when Warren was in one of his dangerous fits and attempted to appease Warren by going up to him and begging him to be more tranquil. This sort of impertinence Warren could not brook and exclaiming, 'You are the blackguard who laughs at the English!' he seized hold of the artist, carried him as if he had been a bundle of straw, and held him out of the window. By the interference of those gentlemen present and the crowd below in the street, Warren was persuaded to carry back the terrified painter into the room. A duel was the consequence, in which the combatants were to fight with pistols until one of them was killed. Warren won the first toss: he levelled, fired, and his adversary fell mortally wounded. This duel was much talked of but no one lamented the result of the duel, for the painter was overbearing and generally disliked by his countrymen as well as by foreigners.

I can scarcely look back to those days of duelling without shuddering. If you looked at a man it was enough: for without having given the slightest offence, cards were exchanged and the odds were that you stood a good chance of being shot, or run through the body, or maimed for life.

PART

FOUR

The Bond Street loungers: (left to right) The Earl of Sefton, the Duke of Devonshire, 'Poodle' Byng, Lord Manners and the Duke of Beaufort.

THE HIGHEST AND BEST SOCIETY

The Regency period – generally reckoned to cover the years between 1810 and 1830 – was a time abounding in contradictions. For example, Britain was looked upon as the most stable country in the world, yet was ruled by a monarch generally supposed to be mad! Britain was also envied as the richest country in the world, yet was stalked by poverty and starvation; and while its government had remained dedicated to freeing Europe from the 'tyranny' of Napoleonic France, it also saw fit to forcibly suppress the personal liberties of its own people.

The contradictions continue with the dukes and lords of the English aristocracy: most received stupendous annual incomes, yet many were in debt; most placed enormous value on elegance, taste, and wit, and yet many cultivated the manners of boxers, coachmen, and jockeys; most took pride in being 'gentlemen' and yet many took pleasure in violent or cruel sports – such as boxing, bear-baiting, hunting, and cock-fights – and spent much of their time gambling, fornicating, or simply getting blind drunk.

It is unsurprising, then, that the man who set the tone for the era, its titular head, the Prince Regent himself, was also a mass of contradictions. George Augustus Frederick, the eldest of George III's fifteen children, was a man of exceptional taste, artistic sensibility, and considerable personal charm: and yet, at the same time, he was also an irresponsible, profligate, lecherous drunk.

By the time he reached adulthood, George, Prince of Wales, was a polished man of some achievement. He was familiar with the classics and with philosophy, was a tolerable mathematician, was reasonably well-read, and could speak fluent French, plus passable German and Italian. He also possessed a pleasing singing voice, and was a proficient cellist (Haydn observing that the prince played 'tolerably well') – he even practised the basics of agriculture in his own private garden at Kew, and baked his own bread. Finally, he was adept in the manly arts of fencing and boxing. No wonder, then, that he was dubbed 'the first gentleman of Europe'. But from this promising bud blossomed the gross, debauched, and dissipated figure lampooned in countless contemporary caricatures: the 'prince of pleasure' who, as the 'georgy porgy, pudding and pie,' of nursery rhyme fame, 'kissed the girls and made them cry'.

And kiss them he did. As prince, and later king, George had a succession of mistresses: perhaps the most celebrated being Mrs Maria Fitzherbert, a widow some six years older than himself, and a devout Catholic, whom he married illegally on 15th December 1785. But George drained the most tears from Caroline of Brunswick, his first cousin, whom he married – this time legally – some ten years later. The marriage was an instant disaster and a year later, after the birth of their daughter, Princess Charlotte (who died in 1817 after a fifty-hour labour resulting in the birth of a stillborn son), the couple separated. But when George gained the throne on the death of his sick father in 1820, Caroline tried to take her rightful place as queen. A horrified George offered her an annuity of £50,000 to relinquish her title and accept a life of exile, but she refused. The government then tried to pass a bill in Parliament, designed to strip Caroline of her rights of queenship and force a divorce upon her, on the grounds of 'licentious behaviour'. By now, however, public support had rallied to the alienated queen's cause and the bill was dropped. Caroline was, however, forcibly barred from attending George's coronation, and she died a few weeks later, apparently of an intestinal obstruction, leaving George free to continue his reign – and his affair with Lady Conyngham – in peace.

George became Regent on 5th February 1811: his father, the German-born George III, having been pronounced insane and placed in a straitjacket. The king had been ill for some time (it is now thought that George III was suffering from porphyria, a rare metabolic disorder), but as he now seemed hopelessly lost in madness, his son, the Prince of Wales, effectively became head of state. Fat, nearly fifty, and generally unpopular with his own subjects – who didn't even see him as an Englishman, but rather, a seventeen-stone European wastrel – George launched the Regency with a grand fête at Carlton House: it was to be a period of elegance, style, artistic achievement – as well as war, oppression, social upheaval – and would last, like George, until 1830.

The Regency was also a time of sharp contrasts. Britain was the birthplace of the industrial revolution, yet on the day George was sworn in as Regent, it was still primarily an agricultural country. Cart tracks linked the many villages, and coach roads linked the few major towns: thus, limited physical mobility perfectly mirrored restricted social mobility in a land of clearly defined social classes. At the top were the aristocrats, Britain's power elite. Hauling huge incomes from land and property, these dukes and lords lived in grand style, like modern heads of state. Many received an annual income in excess of £100,000 per annum, which, when multiplied by a factor of fifty for a rough modern equivalent, gives a figure of £5,000,000. Next came the landed gentry, followed by the so-called 'noveau riche': bankers, merchants, and industrialists thrown up by the industrial revolution. Despite amassing fantastic wealth, these businessmen were frequently looked down upon by their social superiors, some of whom dismissed them as mere 'tradesmen'. Below this burgeoning middle class, came the vast majority of British subjects: an impoverished working class, lucky to earn ten shillings a week, which in modern terms makes about £5,000 per annum. And at the bottom of the heap languished a sizeable underclass of criminals, cut-throats, and convicts.

The stark contrasts of Regency England were perhaps most visible in the capital itself, which was split between the poor East End and the plush West End. London – eleven times bigger than any other British city with a population of just over 1,000,000 souls – was a rumbustious centre of sin, devoid of a police force, and illuminated by oil lamps.

Finally, the Regency was also a time of conflict. Britain's redcoats were not only sent to fight Frenchmen (and of course, Americans), they were also sent to fight their own countrymen, as the nation plunged into political turbulence and civil unrest in the years following Waterloo. For, despite the superabundant riches of the middle and upper classes detailed above, the economic outlook for the average Briton was bleak: especially between the years 1815–1822, when a series of bad harvests and a fall in demand for British goods following the conclusion of the Napoleonic Wars led to severe economic depression. Unemployment, inflation, and poverty increased, the spectre of starvation was raised, and the sufferings of a people deprived of a political voice led to a popular demand for Parliamentary reform. Political 'agitators' and radical 'orators' – such as the celebrated Henry Hunt – began championing the cause of the poor at mass rallies: raising petitions, and organising marches and demonstrations. At the core of the radicals' political agenda were the following demands, embodied in a bill or People's Charter: universal manhood suffrage, equal electoral districts, abolition of property qualifications for MPs, and payment for MPs.

But Lord Liverpool's reactionary Tory government was not listening, and as a consequence, the public mood turned ugly. With no dedicated police force yet in place, soldiers were used for crowd control, and the scene was set for several violent clashes. The worst of these occurred on 16th August 1819, when a crowd of some 60,000 gathered on St Peter's Fields, Manchester, to catch a sight of Henry Hunt. The authorities, fearful of a major insurrection, sent fifty mounted troopers from the local yeomanry to arrest Hunt: but when they were engulfed by the crowd, a detachment of the 15th Hussars – who had last seen action at Waterloo – were sent in. Mayhem followed, and eleven people were killed and at least 400 wounded – women and children among them. The tragedy quickly became known as the 'Peterloo Massacre': a particularly poignant name, as one of the last victims to die of sabre wounds inflicted by the hussars was John Lees, who had fought alongside them as a comrade in the Great Battle.

Despite the contradictions, contrasts, and conflicts, detailed above, however, the popular conception of the Regency is of a time dominated by elegance, style, and grace; best characterized by two types: the Wit and the Dandy. According to E. Beresford Chancellor, in Life in Regency and Early Victorian Times, 'Perhaps the reason why the wits and dandies of this time form so outstanding a feature in London life, is because the mass *of Londoners were not markedly endowed with wit, or capable of initiating or carrying off fashionable modes and fancies. Whatever the reason, the fact remains that the Regency is marked by the cut of a coat or the utterance of an epigram.' While for Venetia Murray, in* High Society, *the dandies, 'were the new elite, the arbiters of fashion, the leaders of the ton.' But if the dandies led society, who led the dandies? No scion of the House of Hanover, that's for sure, but one George Bryan Brummell, acknowledged by all to have attained perfection in the art of elegant dress and manners. According to Carolly Erickson, in* Our Tempestuous Day, *'Brummell's style was an anti-style, a denial of ostentation and self-congratulation.' But Byron put the 'Beau's' case more strongly: 'there are but three great men in the nineteenth century – Brummell, Napoleon, and myself …'*

⧫

⇌• Dining And Cookery In England Fifty Years Ago

England can boast of a Spenser, Shakespeare, Milton, and many other illustrious poets, clearly indicating that the national character of Britons is not deficient in imagination: but we have not had one single masculine inventive genius of the kitchen. It is the probable result of our national antipathy to mysterious culinary compounds that none of the bright minds of England have ventured into the region of scientific cookery. Even in the best houses, when I was a young man, the dinners were wonderfully solid, hot, and stimulating. The menu of a grand dinner was thus composed: Mulligatawny and turtle soups were the first dishes placed before you; a little lower, the eye met with the familiar salmon at one end of the table and the turbot, surrounded by smelts, at the other. The first course was sure to be followed by a saddle of mutton or a piece of roast beef, and then you could take your oath that fowls, tongue, and ham, would as assuredly succeed as darkness after day.

Whilst these never ending *pièces de resistance* were occupying the table, what were called French dishes were, for custom's sake, added to the solid abundance. The French, or side dishes, consisted of very mild but very abortive attempts at Continental cooking, and I have always observed that they met with the neglect and contempt that they merited. The universally-adored and ever-popular boiled potato was eaten with everything, up to the moment when sweets appeared. Our vegetables – the best in the world – were never honoured by an accompanying sauce and generally came to the table cold. A prime difficulty to overcome was the placing on your fork (and finally in your mouth), some half-dozen different eatables that occupied your plate at the same time. For example, your plate would contain, say, a slice of turkey, a piece of stuffing, a sausage, pickles, a slice of tongue, cauliflower, and potatoes. According to habit and custom, a judicious and careful selection from this little bazaar of good things was to be made, with an endeavour to place a portion of each in your mouth at the same moment. In fact, it appeared to me that we used to do all our compound cookery between our jaws.

The dessert – generally ordered at Messrs Granger's or at Owen's in Bond Street, if for a dozen people – would cost at least as many pounds. The wines were chiefly port, sherry, and hock: claret and even Burgundy being then designated 'Poor, thin, washy stuff'. A perpetual thirst seemed to come over people, both men and women, as soon as they had tasted their soup, as from that very moment everybody was taking wine with everybody else till the close of the dinner. And such wine as produced that class of cordiality which frequently wanders into stupefaction. How all this sort of eating and drinking ended was obvious from the prevalence of gout and the necessity of everyone making the pillbox their constant bedroom companion.

🦎· The Prince Regent

When the eldest son of George III assumed the Regency, England was in a state of political transition. The convulsions of the Continent were felt amongst us, the very foundations of European society were shaking, and the social relations of men were rapidly changing. The Regent's natural leanings were towards the Tories: therefore, as soon as he undertook the responsibility of power, he abruptly abandoned the Whigs and retained in office the admirers and partisans of his father's policy. This resolution caused him to have innumerable and inveterate enemies, who never lost an opportunity of attacking his public acts and interfering with his domestic relations.

The Regent was singularly imbued with petty royal pride. He would rather be amiable and familiar with his tailor than agreeable and friendly with the most illustrious of the aristocracy of Great Britain; he would rather joke with a Brummell than admit to his confidence a Norfolk or a Somerset. The Regent was always particularly well-bred in public and showed – if he chose – decidedly good manners. But he very often preferred to address those whom he felt he could patronise. His Royal Highness was as much a victim of circumstances and the child of thoughtless imprudence as the most humble subject of the crown. His unfortunate marriage with a princess of Brunswick originated in his debts, as he married that unhappy lady for £1,000,000 – William Pitt being the contractor! The Princess of Wales married nothing but an association with the Crown of England. If the prince ever seriously loved any woman it was Mrs Fitzherbert, with whom he had appeared at the altar.[1]

Mrs Fitzherbert lived in a magnificent house in Tilney Street, Hyde Park, in great state: her carriages and servants being the same as those H. R. H. made use of. Brummell, who was then on good terms with the prince, called on this lady one day accompanied by his friend Pierrepoint, and found the prince seated on a sofa. The prince, according to the Beau's statement, appeared sullen and evidently annoyed at the visit of the two gentlemen, and on Brummell's taking a pinch of snuff and carelessly placing his box on a small table nearly opposite H. R. H., the prince observed, 'Mr Brummell, the place for your box is in your pocket and not on the table.' Another specimen of H. R. H.'s rudeness may be cited. Lord Barrymore called at Carlton House one day and was ushered into the prince's private

---

1 Maria Anne Fitzherbert (1756–1837), the unlawful wife of George IV by a marriage invalid under the Royal Marriages Act of 1772, was, said M. J. Levy, in *Mistresses of King George IV*, 'Roman Catholic, moral, conventional in outlook, and entirely circumspect in all her relations with men … she was neither witty, outstandingly beautiful, nor exhibitionist … Her beauty was of the homely variety.'

room: on entering he placed his hat on a chair, when H. R. H. observed – in a sarcastic manner – 'My Lord, a well-bred man places his hat under his arm on entering a room and on his head when out of doors.'

In 1816 when I was residing in Paris, I used to have all my clothes made by Staub, in the Rue Richelieu. He had married a very pretty *dame de compagnie* of the celebrated Lady Mildmay and in consequence of this circumstance was patronised and made the fashion by Sir Henry Mildmay and his friends, the dandies.

As I went out a great deal into the world and was every night at some ball or party, I found that knee-breeches were only worn by a few old fogies: trousers and shoes being the usual costume of all the young men of the day. I returned to London with Hervey Aston towards the end of the year and we put up at Fenton's in St James's Street.

I mention the following, somewhat trivial, circumstance to give some notion of the absurd severity in matters of dress and etiquette of Brummell's worthy pupil, the Prince Regent. A few days after my arrival, I received an invitation to a party at Manchester House from Lady Hertford, 'To have the honour of meeting the prince'.

I went there dressed *à la Français,* and quite correctly – as I imagined – with white neckcloth and waistcoat and black trousers, shoes and silk stockings. The prince had dined there and I found him in the octagon-room, surrounded by all the great ladies of the Court. After making my bow and retiring to the further part of the room, I sat down by the beautiful Lady Heathcote, and had been engaged in conversation with her for some time, when Horace Seymour tapped me on the shoulder and said, 'The Great Man' – meaning the prince – 'is very much surprised that you have ventured to appear in his presence without knee-breeches. He considers it as a want of proper respect for him.'

This very disagreeable hint drove me away from Manchester House in a moment, in no very pleasant mood, as may be imagined, and I much fear that I went to bed devoting my royal master to all the infernal gods.

In the morning, being on guard, I mentioned what had occurred –
with some chagrin – to my colonel, Lord Frederick Bentinck, who good-
naturedly told me not to take the matter to heart, as it was really of no
consequence, and he added: 'Depend upon it, Gronow, the prince, who
is a lover of novelty, will wear trousers himself before the year is out, and
then you may laugh at him.'

Lord Frederick proved a true prophet, for in less than a month I had
the satisfaction of seeing 'The finest gentleman in Europe' at a ball at Lady
Cholmondeley's, dressed exactly as I had been at Lady Hertford's, when I
incurred his displeasure, in black trousers and shoes, and Lord Fife, who
was in attendance upon the prince, congratulated me upon the fact that
his royal master had deigned to take example by the young Welshman.

↝· Snuff-Taking

Snuff-taking became generally the fashion in France in the early part of the
reign of Louis XV.[2] In the unfortunate reign of Louis XVI, the beautiful
Marie-Antoinette preferred *bon-bons* to snuff and prided herself on her
bonbonniére, while the old ladies of her court carried snuff-boxes of immense
dimensions with the miniatures of their lovers and children on the lid.

In England, Queen Charlotte, the grandmother of our gracious
queen, was so fond of snuff, that she was the principal cause of making it
fashionable.[3] I recollect having seen Her Majesty on the terrace at Windsor
walking with the king, George III, when, to the great delight of the Eton
boys, she applied her finger and thumb to her gold box, out of which Her
Majesty appeared to have fished a considerable quantity, for the royal nose
was covered with snuff both within and without.

All the ladies in London took a prodigious quantity. I once called
upon the old Duchess of Manchester in Berkeley Square, when she did

---

2 The habit was introduced into England during the reign of Queen Anne (1702–14), by
   soldiers returning from the Wars of the Spanish Succession: prior to this, the English
   had simply smoked their tobacco.

3 Apparently, the queen's excessive use of snuff resulted in her being nicknamed 'Old
   Snuffy' by her family and 'Snuffy Charlotte' by the general populace.

me the honour to offer me a pinch of her best snuff. I was then young but nevertheless accepted the Duchess's offer, and snuffled up a decent quantity, which made me sneeze for at least an hour afterwards, creating much mirth in the drawing room, where many persons were assembled. The Duchess observed how happy she would be if snuff could have the same effect upon her nose as it had upon mine.

George IV always carried a snuff-box, but it appeared to me as if His Majesty took snuff for fashion's sake. He would take the box in his left hand and opening it with his right thumb and forefinger, introduce them into this costly reservoir of snuff, and with a consequential air, convey the same to the nose, but never suffered any to enter: indeed, those who were well acquainted with His Majesty frequently told me he took snuff for effect but never liked it, and allowed all of it to escape from his finger and thumb before it reached the nose.

I should say that the majority of men of fashion at the period I am speaking of carried snuff-boxes. If you knew a man intimately, he would offer you a pinch out of his box, but if others, not so well acquainted wished for a pinch, it was actually refused. In those days of snuff-taking, at the tables of great people and the messes of regiments, snuff-boxes of large proportions followed the bottle and everybody was at liberty to help himself.

It was reported that Brummell, who was celebrated for the beauty of his snuff-boxes and the quality of his snuff, was once dining at the Pavilion with the prince, and incurred his master's heavy displeasure in the following manner. The then Bishop of Winchester, perceiving Brummell's snuff-box within his reach, very naturally took it up and supplied himself with a pinch, upon which Brummell told his servant, who was standing behind his chair, to throw the rest of the snuff into the fire or on the floor. The prince all the while looked daggers: he gave Master Brummell a good wigging the following day and never forgot the insult offered to the bishop. Brummell was then apparently in great favour, but the prince, from that period, began to show his dislike for the beau on several occasions and shortly afterwards quarrelled with him and kept him at arm's length for the remainder of his life.

~• The Prince And Carlton House

One of the meanest and most ugly edifices that ever disfigured London – notwithstanding it was screened by a row of columns – was Carlton House, the residence of the Prince Regent. It was condemned by everybody who possessed taste, and Canova, the sculptor, on being asked his opinion of it, said: 'There are at Rome a thousand buildings more beautiful and whose architecture is in comparison faultless, any one of which would be more suitable for a princely residence than that ugly barn.' This building was constantly under repair but never improved, for no material alterations were made in its appearance. The first step towards improvement should have been to give it a coat of lime-wash, for it was blackened with dust and soot.[4]

Apropos of the alterations: the workmen engaged therein were a great source of annoyance to the prince who, pretending that he did not like to be stared at, objected to their entering by the gateway. It is certain that the Prince Regent kept himself as much aloof as possible from the lower class of his subjects and was annoyed by the natural curiosity of those who hold that as 'a cat may look at a king,' permission for that luxury should not be denied to bipeds.

I recollect that, having called, when on guard, upon Sir Benjamin Bloomfield about the sale of a cob, which he gave me to understand he wanted for the Prince Regent, while conversing we were interrupted by the entrance of the prince, attended by M'Mahon and the eccentric Tommy Tit.[5] His Royal Highness was in an angry humour and blurted

---

4 Carlton House, off Pall Mall, was built at the beginning of the eighteenth century for Henry Boyle, Baron Carlton. George III later granted its use to his son George, Prince of Wales. The house was in poor repair, and in 1783 the prince engaged Henry Holland to reconstruct it. The building work continued for thirty years, but when the prince was crowned George IV he had the place demolished and it was subsequently replaced by John Nash's Carlton House Terrace.

5 Thomas Onslow, second earl of Onslow (1754–1827) was a politician and eccentric crony of the Prince of Wales, whose major service to his royal master was to inform Mrs Fitzherbert (in 1784) that the prince had attempted suicide, and she must save his life. The following year, Onslow mounted guard outside the room where the couple met to marry in secret.

out in his rage, 'I will not allow those maid-servants to look at me when I go in and out, and if I find they do so again, I will have them discharged!' I could hardly believe my ears, that a man born to the highest rank could take umbrage at such pardonable curiosity. But while riding in Hyde Park the next day, I was joined by General Baylie, who, it seemed, had been a spectator of this outburst of wrath: he told me that the prince constantly complained of the servants staring at him and that strict orders had been given to discharge anyone caught repeating the offence.

The Duke of Wellington dined frequently with the Prince Regent who, when he had finished his iced punch and a bottle of sherry, began to be garrulous. The Regent would invariably talk about the battle of Waterloo and speak of the way in which *he* had charged the French with the Household Brigade. Upon one occasion he was so far gone that he had the temerity to tell the duke he had completely bowled over the French cavalry commanded by Marshal Ney. This was too much for the duke to swallow and he said, 'I have heard you, sir, say so before; but I did not witness this marvellous charge. Your Royal Highness must know that the French cavalry are the best in Europe.'

At this same dinner Sir Watkyns William Wynn asked the illustrious duke whether he had a good view of the battle of Waterloo, whereupon the baronet got the following laconic reply, 'I generally like to see what I am about.'

🐜· Spa Fields Riots

The years 1816 and 1817 were a most dangerous period. The spirit of the people of England, exasperated by heavy taxation, the high price of bread, and many iniquitous laws and restrictions – now happily done away with by successive liberal administrations – was of the worst possible nature. In the riots and meetings of those troublous times, the mob really meant mischief and had they been accustomed to the use of arms and well drilled, they might have committed as great excesses as the ruffians of 1793 in France.

On 15th November 1816 a monster meeting was held in Spa Fields, to petition the Prince Regent. Early in the morning of that day, I was sent with a company of the Guards to occupy the prison of Spa Fields and to act, if necessary, in aid and support of the civil power. On our arrival, we found that a troop of horse artillery with their guns had already taken up their position within the yard. We lost no time in making loopholes in the walls, in the event of an attack from without, and made ready for action. The mob, which was not very numerous on our arrival, had by this time increased to an enormous multitude: 60,000 – 70,000 persons must have been present.[6]

Their principal leaders appeared to be Major Cartwright, Gale Jones, and the notorious Henry Hunt, the blacking-maker.[7] The major was an old grey-headed, vulgar-looking man. Hunt was a large, powerfully made fellow, who might have been taken for a butcher. He always wore a white hat, which was (I never knew why) in those days supposed to be an emblem of very advanced liberal or even republican opinions. These two demagogues and two or three more of the leaders of the mob, got into a cart that had been brought up as a sort of tribune or rostrum, from which they harangued the people. More violent and treasonable discourses it was impossible to make, and the huge multitude rent the air with their shouts of applause.

After a time, a magistrate and some constables appeared and summoned the people to disperse. At the same moment a messenger arrived from the prison, who whispered in Hunt's ear that if the mob committed any outrage or made any disturbance, and did not quietly disperse, they would be dealt with by the soldiers, who had orders above all to pick off the ringleaders, should any attack be made upon the prison. This intelligence, conveyed to the gentlemen in the cart by one of their friends, produced a very marked effect. In a very short time they got down – as they seemed to

---

6   This was the first of two public assemblies held at Spa Fields, Clerkenwell, London, and is supposed to have consisted of at least 10,000 peaceful protestors. According to Carolly Erickson, in *Our Tempestuous Day*, 'The purpose of the meeting was to draw up a petition to be carried to the Regent, on behalf of the people of London, by the radical MP Francis Burdett and Henry Hunt, the radicals' most colourful spokesman.'

7   Known also as 'Orator Hunt' (1773–1835), he was the most famous radical speaker of his day. Hunt was also a successful businessman, who produced a range of products, including 'matchless' shoe-blacking, the bottles of which proclaimed his political aims with such radical slogans as: 'Equal Laws, Equal Rights, Annual Parliaments, Universal Suffrage and the Ballot.'

consider themselves in a rather exposed position – declared the meeting at an end and hurried off, leaving the crowd to follow them, which they shortly afterwards did.[8]

Several years after this event, at the time of the Reform Bill, Hunt was elected Member of Parliament for Preston (beating Mr Stanley, the present Earl of Derby) and I was elected for the immaculate borough of Stafford. I well recollect – but cannot describe – the amazement of the blacking-man when I told him one evening, in the smoking-room of the House of Commons, that if any attack had been made upon the prison at Spa Fields, I had given my men orders to pick off Major Cartwright, himself, and one or two more who were in the cart. Hunt was perfectly astonished. He became very red and his eyes seemed to flash fire: 'What, sir! do you mean to say you would have been capable of such an act of barbarity?' 'Yes,' said I, 'and I almost regret you did not give us the opportunity, for your aim that day was to create a revolution and you would have richly deserved the fate which you so narrowly escaped by the cowardice or lukewarmness of your followers.'

⟁· Attempt To Assassinate The Prince Regent

An attempt was made to assassinate the Prince Regent when on his way home from the Houses of Parliament in 1819 but it happily failed.

In the park, opposite Marlborough House, a bullet was fired from an airgun by a man concealed in one of the trees, who escaped. This occurred when I was on duty at the Horse Guards, marching across the park with what was commonly called the Tilt Guard and I remember it was anything but pleasant to get through the mob of blackguards who were ripe for

---

8 According to the Newgate Calendar, Hunt addressed the crowd – which had been requested to remain tranquil – from the window of a local pub, 'and after declaiming in his usual manner about the corruption of the government and the distresses of the country, concluded by moving his resolutions; one of which was that the assembly should meet again on the Monday fortnight following, in order to hear the Prince Regent's answer to the petition.' Interestingly, Gronow fails to mention this meeting, which took place on 2nd December 1816, and which degenerated into a riot when some 200 protestors – out of a crowd of around 20,000 – broke into a local gunsmith's shop and went on the rampage.

mischief. The Life Guards, who escorted the prince, evinced great want of energy on the occasion. The officer commanding the troop, when he saw the danger, should have commanded his men to charge and clear the way. Such was my opinion then, and I am persuaded from all that I have witnessed since, that the wisest plan upon such occasions, is to take the initiative and act promptly. The fact of this attempt having been made was doubted at the time by the public at large, but I can speak from my personal knowledge that a shot was fired and it was aimed at the royal carriage.[9]

⁓• Escapade Of An Officer Of The 3rd Foot Guards

It is nearly fifty years since a young officer in the 3rd Guards, smitten with the charms of Lady Betty Charteris, who was remarkable for her beauty and attainments, determined at all hazards to carry her off and marry her. Her father put a stop to any legitimate, straightforward wooing, by forbidding her to encourage the attentions of the young officer, who was too poor to maintain her in the position in which she had been brought up. When the London season was over, the family left for Scotland, and my friend, Andrew C __, decided on following his lady-love. Andrew was young, handsome, romantic, and sentimental: but a brave fellow, and had fought gallantly at Waterloo. After consulting several of his intimate friends, who recommended perseverance, he determined to further his scheme by disguising himself. So, with the aid of a black wig and a suit of seedy clothes, he engaged the services of an Italian organ-grinder, and took his place beside him on one of the Edinburgh coaches.

---

9 It is generally accepted that this incident took place on 28th January 1817. Saul David, in *Prince of Pleasure*, states: 'Lord James Murray, who was accompanying the Regent, spoke of "two small holes made by a sharp blow of some sort within one inch of each other, through an uncommonly thick plate glass window." He was convinced that they had been made by someone firing an airgun, though "no bullets were found in the coach, nor was any person in it hurt." 'No one was ever arrested in connection with this 'attack', but the government convinced itself that the country was on the brink of revolution and passed a series of repressive laws – known as The Six Acts – in an effort to suppress political agitation, public gatherings, and the possession of firearms and 'seditious' literature.

In the course of a few days the pair arrived at a village close to the mansion of the lady's father, and a correspondence was carried on between the lovers. They met, and after a great many urgent entreaties on the part of the enamoured swain, a day was arranged for the elopement. Andrew next gained over the head gardener, by stating that he had just arrived from Holland, and was up to the latest dodges in tulip-growing, then a mania in England. By this means he contrived to be constantly on the premises, and to obtain frequent interviews with the charming Lady Betty.

The day fixed at length arrived and the organ-grinder (then a rarity in Scotland) was introduced on the scene: his sprightly airs fascinated the servants, who thronged to listen to him, and meanwhile a postchaise and four was driven up, out of sight of the house, according to a previous understanding between the lovers, who were ready for instant flight. Unluckily, there was an excessively vigilant governess in attendance on Lady Betty, and at the moment when affairs seemed most prosperous, this duenna was at her post at the young lady's side in the garden. Andrew, feeling that everything depended on some decisive action, suddenly appeared, and ejaculating, 'Now or never!' caught hold of his dulcinea's arm and attempted to hurry in the direction of the chaise. The dragon interposed and clung to the young lady, screaming for assistance: her cries brought out the servants, the enraged father, and the inmates of the house to her assistance, and poor Andrew and the organ-man with his monkey were ejected from the premises.

The young Guardsman, however, soon got over the sorrow caused by the failure of his scheme: but the nickname of 'Merry Andrew', bestowed on him by his brother officers, stuck to him afterwards.

⚮· 'King' Allen

The late Viscount Allen, commonly called 'King' Allen, was a well-known character in London for many years. He was a tall, stout and pompous-looking personage, remarkably well got up, with an invariably new-looking hat and well-polished boots. His only exercise and usual walk was from White's to Crockford's and from Crockford's to White's.

Who in this ponderous old man would have recognised the gallant youth who, as an ensign in the Guards, led on his men with incredible energy across the ravine at Talavera where, if the great duke had not sent the 48th Regiment to their assistance, very little more would have been heard of 'King' Allen and his merry men? But one of the most famous dandies of his day was not fated thus to perish, and he was preserved for thirty years after the great battle, to swagger down Bond Street or lounge on the sunny side of Pall Mall, to become an *arbiter elegantiarum* [judge of elegance] amongst the tailors and a Mæcenas at the opera and play.[10]

To render the 'King' happy, one little item was wanting: money. His estates – if he ever had any – had long passed from him and he had much difficulty in making the two ends meet. When, for economy's sake, he was obliged to retire for a short time to Dublin, he had a very large door in Merrion Square with an almost equally large brass plate, on which his name was engraved in letters of vast size. But it was very much doubted whether there was any house behind it. He was a great diner out, and one spiteful old lady, whom he had irritated by some uncivil remarks, told him that his title was as good as board and wages to him.

Strange to say, this *mauvais sujet* was a great friend of the late Sir Robert Peel, when Chief Secretary for Ireland, and on one occasion, when they were proceeding in an open carriage to dine with a friend a few miles from Dublin, in passing through a village, they had the misfortune to drive over the oldest inhabitant, an ancient beldam, who was generally stationed on the bridge. A large mob gathered round the carriage and as Peel and the Tory government were very unpopular at the period to which I refer, the mob began to grow abusive and cast threatening and ominous looks at the occupants of the barouche: when the 'King', with a coolness and self-possession worthy of Brummell, rose up, displaying an acre of white waistcoat, and called out, 'Now, postboy, go on, and don't drive over any more old women.' The mob, awe-struck by 'King' Allen's

---

10 Gaius Maecenas (70–8BC) was political advisor to Caesar Augustus and a leading sponsor and friend to aspiring poets. His name has come to mean any wealthy patron of the Arts.

majestic deportment, retired, and 'The industrious and idle apprentices' went on their way rejoicing.

The 'King' was not a very good-natured person, and as he had a strong inclination to – and some talent for – sarcasm, he made himself many enemies. To give an idea of his 'style': when the statue of George III was erected in front of Ransom's banking-house, Mr Williams, one of the partners (commonly known by the name of 'Swell Bill'), petitioned the Woods and Forests to remove that work of art, as it collected a crowd of little boys who were peculiarly facetious on the subject of the pig-tail of that obstinate but domestic monarch, and otherwise obstructed business. Lord Allen, meeting Williams at White's, said: 'I should have thought the erection of the statue rather an advantage to you because, while you were standing idle at your own shop door, it would prevent you seeing the crowds hurrying to the respectable establishment of Messrs Coutts & Co., close by in the Strand.'

The 'King' did not posses much wit but no one could say more disagreeable things at the most disagreeable moment. I remember his setting down the late Lady N__, daughter-in-law of a celebrated legal functionary of that name, in rather an amusing manner. She was a vulgar Irish grazier's daughter, extremely plain, and clipped the king's English in a vain attempt to conceal a mellifluous king's county brogue. After passing many years in Rutland Square, Dublin, she suddenly found herself a countess with a large income. Her first step after this accession of dignity and fortune was to start for London, where she affected to have passed her life. On meeting Lord Allen soon after her arrival, she extended one finger of her little fat hand and in a drawling, affected tone of voice said, 'My Lard Alleen, how long have you been in London?' 'Forty years, ma'am!' growled out the 'King.'

Lord Allen greatly resembled in later life an ancient grey parrot, both in the aquiline outline of his features, and his peculiar mode of walking with one foot crossed over the other in a slow and wary manner. He was a regular cockney and very seldom left London. But on one occasion, when he had gone down with Alvanley to Dover, for the sake of his health, and complained to his facetious friend that he could get no sleep, Alvanley ordered a coach to drive up and down in front of the inn window all night and made the boots call out, in imitation of the London watchmen of that day, 'Half-past two, and a stormy night!' The well-known rumble of the wheels and the dulcet tones of the boots had the desired effect: the 'King' passed excellent nights and was soon able to return to his little house in South Street with renewed health and spirits.

Lord Allen was at last obliged to leave London, after coming to an understanding with his creditors, and after passing some time at Cadiz, died at Gibraltar in 1843, when his title became extinct.

≫• Lord Alvanley

From the time of Good Queen Bess, when the English language first began to assume somewhat of its present form, idiom, and mode of expression, to the days of our most gracious sovereign Queen Victoria, every age has had its punsters, humorists, and eloquent conversationalists: but I much doubt whether the year 1789 did not produce the greatest wit of modern times, in the person of William Lord Alvanley.[11]

After receiving a very excellent and careful education, Alvanley entered the Coldstream Guards at an early age and served with distinction at Copenhagen and in the Peninsula. But being in possession of a large fortune, he left the army, gave himself up entirely to the pursuit of pleasure, and became one of the principal dandies of the day. With the brilliant talents that he possessed, he might have attained to the highest eminence in any line of life he had embraced.

Not only was Alvanley considered the wittiest man of his day in England, but during his residence in France and tours through Russia and other countries, he was universally admitted to possess – not only the greatest wit and humour – but *l'esprit français* in its highest perfection, and no greater compliment could be paid him by foreigners than this. He was one of the rare examples (particularly rare in the days of the dandies,

---

11 William Arden (1789–1849), 2nd Baron Alvanley. His first claim to fame was as an athlete; in 1808 he ran a mile in under six minutes, winning a bet of 50 guineas. Alvanley 'was ultimately to inherit Brummell's reputation for wit though not for elegance.'

who were generally sour and spiteful) of a man combining brilliant wit and repartee with the most perfect good nature. His manner, above all, was irresistible, and the slight lisp, which might have been considered as a blemish, only added piquancy and zest to his sayings.

In appearance he was about the middle height and well and strongly built – though he latterly became somewhat corpulent. He excelled in all manly exercises, was a hard rider to hounds, and was what those who do not belong to the upper ten thousand call 'a good plucked one'. His face had somewhat of the rotund form and smiling expression, which characterise the jolly friars one meets with in Italy. His hair and eyes were dark and he had a very small nose, to which, after deep potations, his copious pinches of snuff had some difficulty in finding their way, and were in consequence rather lavishly bestowed upon his florid cheek. He resided in Park Street, St James's, and his dinners there and at Melton were considered to be the best in England. He never invited more than eight people and insisted upon having the somewhat expensive luxury of an apricot tart on the sideboard the whole year round.

Alvanley was a good speaker, and having made some allusion to O'Connell in rather strong terms in the House of Lords, the latter very coarsely and unjustly denounced him in a speech he made in the House of Commons, as a bloated buffoon. Alvanley thereupon called out the Liberator, who would not meet him but excused himself by saying, 'There is blood already on this hand,' alluding to his fatal duel with d'Esterre.[12]

Alvanley then threatened O'Connell with personal chastisement. Upon this, Morgan O'Connell, a very agreeable, gentlemanlike man, who had been in the Austrian service and whom I knew well, said he would take his father's place. A meeting was accordingly agreed upon at Wimbledon Common. Alvanley's second was Colonel George Dawson Damer. Colonel

---

12 Daniel O'Connell (1775–1847), the Irish nationalist leader known as the Liberator, fought a pistol duel with merchant John D'Esterre on 1st February 1815. The duel took place at Bishop's Court, Co. Kildare, and resulted in the latter's death: something O'Connell bitterly regretted, leading him to renounce duelling.

Hodges acted for Morgan O'Connell. Several shots were fired without effect and the seconds then interfered and put a stop to further hostilities.[13]

On their way home in a hackney coach, Alvanley said, 'What a clumsy fellow O'Connell must be to miss such a fat fellow as I am! He ought to practise at a haystack to get his hand in.' When the carriage drove up to Alvanley's door, he gave the coachman a sovereign. 'Jarvey' [slang for a coachman] was profuse in his thanks and said, 'It's a great deal for only having taken your Lordship to Wimbledon.' 'No my good man,' said Alvanley, 'I give it you not for taking me but for bringing me back.'

𝕳· Ball Hughes

I was at Eton with my late friend Ball Hughes,[14] whose recent death was so much lamented in Paris. He was known at Eton by the name of Ball only, but the year before he came of age, he took the additional name of Hughes: his uncle, Admiral Hughes, having left him the fortune he had amassed during his command of the fleet on the Indian seas and which was supposed to be not less than £40,000 a year. But Hughes entered the army early in life, his uncle having bought him a commission in the 7th Hussars and made him some allowance. He was a great imitator of the colonel of his regiment, the Earl of Uxbridge, afterwards Marquis of Anglesey, whom he took as a model for his coats, hats, and boots. Indeed everything that his noble commander said or did was law to him. Hughes was a remarkably handsome man and made a considerable figure in the best society. His manners were excellent. He was a thoroughly amiable, agreeable fellow, and universally popular.

When he came into his fortune, he was considered a great match by all the women in London. He fell desperately in love with Lady Jane Paget, the daughter of his colonel and the marriage-settlements were all arranged,

---

13 Morgan O'Connell (1804–1885), fought his duel with Alvanley at Chalk Farm, east of Primrose Hill, London, on 4th May 1835: two shots each were exchanged, but neither man was injured.

14 Edward Ball Hughes (1799–1863). Ball Hughes was notoriously reckless with money, and once lost £45,000 in a single night, gambling at Wattier's Club.

but unluckily for the disappointed lover, Lady Jane, at the last moment, gave a most decided negative and the match was broken off. Ball was not long disconsolate, but looking around him, fixed his attention upon the lovely Miss Floyd, who afterwards married Sir Robert Peel. Finding his attentions unacceptable in that quarter, he proposed to Lady Caroline Churchill – afterwards Lady Caroline Pennant – but here he was refused. This, however, did not prevent him from being considered an eligible match by a great many mothers, who diligently sought his society. He was courted, followed, and admired by everyone who had daughters to dispose of: but unfortunately for him, the young ladies, having heard of his numerous disappointments, were not ready to unite their fate with a man whose rejected addresses were so well known. The Golden Ball, as he was called, continued nevertheless, to make his appearance everywhere. He was devoted to female society: no dinner, ball, picnic, or party, was complete unless the popular millionaire formed one of the social circle.

Ball Hughes' first step, on entering into possession of his fortune, was to employ Mr Wyatt, the architect, to furnish a mansion for him in Brook Street. No expense was spared to make it as near perfection as possible. Wyatt had a *carte-blanche* and bought for him buhl furniture, rich hangings, statues, bronzes, and works of art to an extent that made an inroad even upon his wealth.

A beautiful Spanish *danseuse* named Mercandotti arrived about this time in London, under the patronage of Lord Fife. She was then only fifteen years of age and by some she was believed to be his daughter, by others only his *protégée*. At Barcelona she was considered inimitable; at Madrid she gained great applause; in Seville she acquired immense reputation; and by the time the lovely girl reached London, great curiosity was excited to see the new candidate for public favour at the King's Theatre, where she was engaged for the season at £800. The new *débutante* met with complete success and was pronounced divine. All the dandies who had the *entrée* behind the scenes surrounded her and paid her homage, and more than one scion of the fashionable world offered to surrender his liberty for life to the fascinating dancer. Ebers, then manager of the theatre, was pestered from morning to night by young men of fashion anxious to obtain an introduction to Mademoiselle Mercandotti, but they were invariably referred by the *impresario* to Lord Fife.

One night, 8th March 1823, the house was enormously crowded by an audience eager to see the favourite in the then popular ballet by Auber, *Alfred*, when just before the curtain drew up, the manager came forward and expressed his regret that Mademoiselle Mercandotti had disappeared and he had been unable to discover where she had gone. Knowing ones, however, guessed she had been carried off by the Golden Ball, whose advances had been very favourably received and who had evidently made a strong impression upon the damsel. And a few days after, the *Morning Post* announced that a marriage had taken place between a young man of large fortune and one of the most remarkable dancers of the age. The persons present at the marriage were the mother of the bride, Mr Ebers, and Lord Fife. The honeymoon was passed at Oatlands, which the happy bridegroom had shortly before purchased from the Duke of York. Ainsworth wrote the following epigram on this event:

'The fair damsel is gone; and no wonder at all,
That, bred to the dance, she is gone to a ball.'

ᘓ· The Late Mrs Bradshaw (Maria Tree)
The two Miss Trees, Maria and Ellen (the latter now Mrs Kean), were the favourites of the Bath stage for many seasons before they became leading stars in London. Miss Ellen Tree made her first appearance in a grand entertainment called *The Cataract Of The Ganges,* in a magnificent car drawn by six horses. Her beauty made a deep impression on the audience, which was naturally increased by her subsequent exhibition of great talents.

Miss Maria Tree was much admired as a vocalist and her Viola, in *Twelfth Night,* was one of the most popular performances of the day. Mr Bradshaw[15] became desperately enamoured of her during her engagement

---

15 Widower James Bradshaw, the wealthy tea merchant and MP for Canterbury.

in London, and having learned that she was about to go by the mail coach to Birmingham, where she was about to perform her principal characters, thought it a favourable opportunity of enjoying her society: so he sent his servant to secure him a place by the mail, under the name of Tomkins. At the appointed time for departure Mr Bradshaw was at the office and jumping into the coach was soon whirled away. But great was his disappointment at finding that the fair object of his admiration was not a fellow-passenger. He was not consoled by discovering that there were two mails, the one the Birmingham mail and the other the Birmingham and Manchester, and that whilst he was journeying by the latter, Miss Tree was travelling in the other.

On arriving at Birmingham, early in the morning, he left the coach and stepped into the hotel, determined to remain there and go to the theatre on the following evening. He went to bed and slept late the following day, but on waking he remembered that his trunk – with all his money – had gone on to Manchester, and that he was without the means of paying his way. Seeing the Bank of Birmingham opposite the hotel, he went over and explained his position to one of the partners, giving his own banker's address in London and showing letters addressed to him as Mr Bradshaw. Upon this he was told that with such credentials he might have a loan, and the banker said he would write the necessary letter and cheque and send the money over to him at the hotel. Mr Bradshaw, pleased with this kind of attention, sat himself down comfortably to breakfast in the coffee-room.

According to promise, the cashier made his appearance at the hotel and asked the waiter for Mr Bradshaw: 'No such gentleman here,' was the reply. 'Oh yes, he came by the London mail.' 'No sir, no one came but Mr Tomkins, who was booked as inside passenger to Manchester.' The cashier was dissatisfied, but the waiter added, 'Sir, you can look through the window of the coffee-room door and see the gentleman yourself.' On doing so, he beheld the supposed Mr Tomkins – *alias* Mr Bradshaw – and immediately returned to the bank, telling what he himself had heard and seen. The banker went over to the hotel, had a consultation with the landlord, and it was determined that a watch should be placed upon the suspicious person who had two names and no luggage, and who was booked to Manchester but had stopped at Birmingham.

The landlord then summoned 'Boots', a little lame fellow of the most ludicrous appearance, and pointing to the gentleman in the coffee-room, told him his duty for the day was to follow him wherever he went and never to lose sight of him; but above all to take care that he did not get away. 'Boots' nodded assent and immediately mounted guard. Mr Bradshaw having taken his breakfast and read the papers, looked at his watch and sallied forth to see something of the goodly town of Birmingham. He was much surprised at observing a little odd-looking man surveying him most attentively and watching his every movement, stopping whenever he stopped and evidently taking a deep interest in all he did. At last, observing that he was the object of this incessant *espionage,* and finding that he had a shilling left in his pocket, he hailed one of the coaches that ran short distances in those days when omnibuses were not. This, however, did not suit little 'Boots', who went up to him and insisted that he must not leave the town.

Mr Bradshaw's indignation was naturally excessive and he immediately returned to the hotel, where he found a constable ready to take him before the mayor as an imposter and swindler. He was compelled to appear before his worship and had the mortification of being told that unless he could give some explanation, he must be content with a night's lodging in a house of detention. Mr Bradshaw had no alternative but to send to the fair charmer of his heart to identify him – which she most readily did – as soon as rehearsal was over. Explanations were then entered into, but he was forced to give the reason for being in Birmingham, which of course made a due impression on the lady's heart and led to that happy result of their interview: a marriage which resulted in the enjoyment of mutual happiness for many years.[16]

♔ Sally Brooke

There was a celebrated beauty who in my day made a conspicuous figure both in London and on the Continent. Miss Brooke – or as she was more

---

16 The couple produced a single child, named Harriet Maria; Bradshaw died in 1847.

generally called, Sally Brooke – was the daughter of a beneficed clergyman: she had agreeable manners, her education had been highly finished, and she always mingled in the best men's circles. For some reason, which never was known, she quitted her parents' roof and came to London, where she created a considerable impression. She was most particularly noticed by the Prince of Wales and consequently well received by those who basked in princely favour. Not a word, however, was ever breathed against her honour, and she was always looked upon as a model of unimpeachable veracity. Her beauty was such that she became the object of general admiration and her portrait was taken by the first painters of the day. *The Hebe* by Srœling, engraved by Heath, remains to enable the world to form some idea of the matchless charms of the original. Her figure was perfection and the sculptor would have been delighted to have obtained such a model. From whence she derived her income was always a mystery. A silly story was for a moment circulated that a person of the name of Bouverie, commonly called 'The Commissioner', had succeeded in captivating her: this, however, soon died away. Whatever may have been her resources, she kept up a good establishment in Green Street and lived always like a lady but without much show. Her house was the rendezvous of the first men in London, but to her own sex she was distant and reserved, never admitting any female to her familiarity.

On one occasion, Miss Brooke dined at the house of a noble marquis, where some of the fashionable young men of the day were invited to meet her. Mr Christopher Nugent, a nephew of the celebrated Burke, was most assiduous in his attentions and begged permission to pay her a visit: the request was granted and a day and an hour named. Some of the party present incidentally mentioned this engagement in the presence of the widow of a Mr Harrison, a lady who had access to the best circles in consequence of her remarkable beauty, and who had some right to place Mr Nugent on the list of her admirers. Jealous of her rival, the widow dressed herself as a boy, knocked at the door in Green Street and was admitted into the presence of Miss Brooke, who was reclining on her sofa, whilst Nugent was on his knees before her. The distinguished lady, finding her lover in such a position, rushed upon him, seized a knife, and plunged it into his breast – fortunately without inflicting a mortal wound. Whatever might have been expected when this fact was generally known, it was soon believed that love had healed the wounds which jealousy inflicted: for Nugent and the lovely widow were soon seen walking together in familiar conversation in Hyde Park.

After being the admiration of the world of fashion for several seasons, Sally Brooke, seeing wrinkles coming into her once Hebe-like face, determined to leave scenes where she no longer reigned as the queen of beauty (but found other and fresher forms admired) and went to Baden. There some scoundrels having robbed her of all she possessed, she left the place and arrived at the Hôtel du Palais Royal at Strasbourg, where she remained some years, 'the world forgetting, by the world forgot.' A dropsical disease ravaged her once symmetrical form and she died in a land of strangers. Her landlord nobly defrayed the expenses of her funeral, although she was already much indebted to him. Her family, however, liquidated her debts. Her remains repose in the city of Strasbourg and her tomb is one of the memorials of human vanity.

☙· Beau Brummell

Amongst the curious freaks of fortune there is none more remarkable in my memory than the sudden appearance, in the highest and best society in London, of a young man whose antecedents warranted a much less conspicuous career. I refer to the famous Beau Brummell.[17] We have innumerable instances of soldiers, lawyers, and men of letters, elevating themselves from the most humble stations and becoming the companions of princes and lawgivers, but there are comparatively few examples of men obtaining a similarly elevated position simply from their attractive personal appearance and fascinating manners. Brummell's father, who was a steward to one or two large estates, sent his son George to Eton. He was endowed with a handsome person and distinguished himself at Eton as the

---

17 George Bryan Brummell (1778–1840).

best scholar, the best boatman, and the best cricketer, and more than all, he was supposed to possess the comprehensive excellences that are represented by the familiar term of 'Good Fellow'. He made many friends amongst the scions of good families, by whom he was considered a sort of Crichton[18] and his reputation reached a circle over which reigned the celebrated Duchess of Devonshire. At a grand ball given by her Grace, George Brummell, then quite a youth, appeared for the first time in such elevated society. He immediately became a great favourite with the ladies and was asked by all the dowagers to as many balls and *soirées* as he could attend.

At last the Prince of Wales sent for Brummell and was so much pleased with his manner and appearance, that he gave him a commission in his own regiment, the 10th Hussars.[19] Unluckily, Brummell, soon after joining his regiment, was thrown from a horse at a grand review at Brighton, when he broke his classical Roman nose. This misfortune, however, did not affect the fame of the beau, and although his nasal organ had undergone a slight transformation, it was forgiven by his admirers, since the rest of his person remained intact. When we are prepossessed by the attractions of a favourite, it is not a trifle that will dispel the illusion, and Brummell continued to govern society, in conjunction with the Prince of Wales.

He was remarkable for his dress, which was generally conceived by himself, the execution of his sublime imagination being carried out by that superior genius, Mr Weston, tailor, of Old Bond Street. The Regent sympathised deeply with Brummell's labours to arrive at the most attractive and gentlemanly mode of dressing the male form, at a period when fashion had placed at the disposal of the tailor the most hideous material that could possibly tax his art. The coat may have a long tail or a short tail, a high collar or a low collar, but it will always be an ugly garment. The modern hat may be spread out at the top, or narrowed, whilst the brim may be

---

18 A reference to the sixteenth century Scottish polymath, James Crichton of Eliock and Cluny, famous for his many achievements in a variety of fields.

19 Brummell's military duties largely involved accompanying the prince to numerous social engagements. He quit the regiment in 1798 in order to avoid doing garrison duty in Manchester, a post he felt was beneath his dignity.

turned up or turned down, made a little wider or a little more narrow: it
is still inconceivably hideous. Pantaloons and Hessian boots were the least
objectionable features of the costume that the imagination of a Brummell
and the genius of a royal prince were called upon to modify or change.
The hours of meditative agony that each dedicated to the odious fashions
of the day have left no monument, save the coloured caricatures, in which
these illustrious persons have appeared.

Brummell, at this time, besides being the companion of the prince, was
very intimate with the dukes of Rutland, Dorset, and Argyle, Lords Sefton,
Alvanley, and Plymouth. In the zenith of his popularity he might be seen at
the bay window of White's Club, surrounded by the lions of the day, laying
down the law, and occasionally indulging in those witty remarks for which
he was famous. His house in Chapel Street corresponded with his personal
get up: the furniture was in excellent taste and the library contained the
best works of the best authors of every period and of every country. His
canes, his snuff-boxes, his Sèvres china, were exquisite. His horses and
carriage were conspicuous for their excellence. And in fact the superior
taste of a Brummell was discoverable in everything that belonged to him.

But the reign of the king of fashion, like all other reigns, was not
destined to continue forever. Brummell warmly espoused the cause of Mrs
Fitzherbert and this of course offended the Prince of Wales. I refer to the
period when His Royal Highness had abandoned that beautiful woman for
another favourite. A coldness then ensued between the prince and his *protégé*
and finally the mirror of fashion was excluded from the royal presence.

A curious accident brought Brummell again to the dinner-table of his
royal patron. He was asked one night at White's to take a hand at whist,
when he won from George Harley Drummond £20,000. This circumstance
having been related by the Duke of York to the Prince of Wales, the beau
was again invited to Carlton House. At the commencement of the dinner,
matters went off smoothly, but Brummell, in his joy at finding himself
with his old friend became excited and drank too much wine. His Royal
Highness – who wanted to pay off Brummell for an insult he had received at
Lady Cholmondeley's ball, when the beau, turning towards the prince, said

to Lady Worcester, 'Who is your fat friend?'[20] – had invited him to dinner merely out of a desire for revenge. The prince therefore pretended to be affronted by Brummell's hilarity and said to his brother, the Duke of York: 'I think we had better order Mr Brummell's carriage before he gets drunk.' Whereupon he rang the bell and Brummell left the royal presence.

Brummell's latter days of were clouded with mortification and penury. He retired to Calais, where he kept up a ludicrous imitation of his past habits. At last he got himself named consul at Caen, but he afterwards lost the appointment, and eventually died insane and in abject poverty at Calais.[21]

🐜· Lord Byron

I knew very little of Lord Byron[22] personally but lived much with two of his intimate friends, Scrope Davies and Wedderburn Webster, from whom I heard many anecdotes of him. I regret that I remember so few and wish that I had written down those told me by poor Scrope Davies, one of the most agreeable men I ever met.

When Byron was at Cambridge he was introduced to Scrope Davies by their mutual friend, Mathews, who afterwards drowned in the River

---

20 Several versions of this famous incident exist: for instance, Hubert Cole, in *Beau Brummell*, has the dandy saying, 'Ah, Alvanley, who is your fat friend?'; while Philip Carter, in his article on Brummell in the *Oxford Dictionary of Biography*, gives the following: 'Promenading with Lord Moira in St James Street, Brummell had encountered the prince who greeted Moira but ignored his companion. "Pray who is your fat friend?" asked Brummell in a sufficiently loud voice on resuming their walk.'

21 A desperate financial situation, exacerbated by gambling, obliged Brummell to decamp for Calais on 16th May 1816. Further money troubles forced him to accept the post of consul for the department of Calvados. Consequently, in September 1830, he took up residency at the Hôtel d'Angleterre in Caen. Two years later, Brummell was dismissed after repeated complaints concerning the insignificance of his post. Now unemployed, Brummell had little chance of paying off his debts, and in April 1835 he was arrested and gaoled for failing to repay an outstanding sum of 15,000 francs. By this time, he had suffered three strokes, and was reduced to living on handouts from the shopkeepers of Caen. He ended his days in the Bon Sauveur asylum, where he died on 30th March 1840 at the age of sixty-two. Brummell was buried in Caen's protestant cemetery.

22 George Gordon Noel, sixth Baron Byron (1788–1824).

Cam.[23] After Mathews' death, Davies became Byron's particular friend and was admitted to his rooms at all hours. Upon one occasion he found the poet in bed with his hair *en papillote* [in curling papers], upon which Scrope cried, 'Ha, ha! Byron, I have at last caught you acting the part of Sleeping Beauty.' Byron, in a rage, exclaimed, 'No, Scrope, the part of a damn fool, you should have said.' 'Well, then, anything you please, but you have succeeded admirably in deceiving your friends, for it was my conviction that your hair curled naturally.' 'Yes, naturally, every night,' returned the poet, 'but do not, my dear Scrope, let the cat out of the bag, for I am as vain of my curls as a girl of sixteen.'

When in London, Byron used to go to Manton's shooting-gallery in Davies Street, to try his hand, as he said, at a wafer. Wedderburn Webster was present when the poet, intensely delighted at his own skill, boasted to Joe Manton[24] that he considered himself the best shot in London. 'No, my Lord,' replied Manton, 'not the best, but your shooting today was respectable.' Whereupon Byron waxed wroth and left the shop in a violent passion.[25]

Lords Byron, Yarmouth, Pollington, Mountjoy, Wallscourt, Blandford, Captain Burges, Jack Bouverie, and myself were in 1814 – and for several years afterwards – amongst the chief and most frequenters of this well-known shooting-gallery and frequently shot at the wafer for considerable sums of money. Manton was allowed to enter the betting list and he generally backed me.

Byron lived a great deal at Brighton, his house being opposite the Pavilion. He was fond of boating and was generally accompanied by a lad,

---

23 The future poet had entered Trinity College in 1805, but as was usual for a an undergraduate aristocrat, rarely attended lectures, spending most of his time swimming, riding, and refurbishing his rooms: this latter occupation disposing of his allowance and plunging him into debt with moneylenders.

24 Joseph Manton (1766–1835) was the acknowledged 'king of the gun makers', whose weapons were much sought after.

25 Captain Ross was generally regarded as the best shot of the day, with Gronow himself coming a close second.

who was said to be a girl in boy's clothes. This report was confirmed to me by Webster, who was then living at Brighton. The vivid description of the page in *Lara,* no doubt gave some plausibility to this oft-told tale. I myself witnessed the dexterous manner in which Byron used to get into his boat, for, while standing on the beach, I once saw him vault into it with the agility of a harlequin, in spite of his lame foot.

On one occasion, whilst his lordship was dining with a few of his friends in Charles Street, Pall Mall, a letter was delivered to Scrope Davies, which required an immediate answer. Scrope, after reading its contents, handed it to Lord Byron. It was thus worded:

> *'My dear Scrope, lend me 500l. for a few days; the funds are shut for the dividends, or I should not have made this request.*
>
> G. *Brummell'*

The reply was:

> *'My dear Brummell, all my money is locked up in the funds.*
>
> *Scrope Davies.'*

This was just before Brummell's escape to the Continent.

I have frequently asked Scrope Davies his private opinion of Lord Byron and invariably received the same answer: that he considered Byron very agreeable and clever, but vain, overbearing, conceited, suspicious, and jealous. Byron hated Palmerston but liked Peel and thought that the whole world ought to be constantly employed in admiring his poetry and himself. He never could write a poem or a drama without making himself its hero, and he was always the subject of his own conversation.

During one of Hobhouse's visits to Byron, at his villa near Genoa, and whilst they were walking in his garden, his Lordship suddenly turned upon his guest and *apropos* of nothing, exclaimed, 'Now, I know, Hobhouse, you are looking at my foot.' Upon which Hobhouse kindly replied, 'My dear Byron, nobody thinks of or looks at anything but your head.'

During Lord Byron's sojourn at Lisbon, he was much amused with Dan Mackinnon's various funny stories. Upon one occasion Dan's time was entirely taken up by presenting women with toothbrushes, a supply of which he had received by the packet from London. Opposite his quarters there lived two very pretty Portuguese ladies who, unmindful of Dan's proximity (and of the fact that his windows commanded a view of their chamber), dressed, undressed, and went through their morning ablutions and toilet. Dan's astonishment was great when he perceived that the fair ones never brushed their teeth, and he lost no time in sending his servant with two toothbrushes in paper, well perfumed and sealed up. The ladies opened the packet and appeared delighted with the present: but judge of Mackinnon's horror in beholding those dainty creatures perseveringly brushing their raven locks with the tiny brushes!

Lord Byron was a great admirer of well-formed hands: he preferred a pretty hand to a pretty face. He was asked whether he admired pretty feet: his answer was that he never went so low. 'And as for teeth,' said he, 'a blackamoor has as white a set of teeth as the fairest lady in the land.' His Lordship added, 'A Frenchman thinks very little of the teeth, face, or colour of the hair, provided a woman put on her cashmere veil in a graceful manner and is well-shod, then he is in raptures with her.'

☞· Mrs Mary Anne Clarke

Our army, despite its defects, was nevertheless infinitely better administered at home when I joined it than it had been a few years before, owing principally to the inquiry that had taken place in the House of Commons, relative to the bribery and corruption that had crept in, and which had been laid open by the confessions of a female – who created no small sensation in those days – and who eventually terminated her extraordinary career, not very long since, in Paris.

The squibs fired off by Mrs Mary Anne Clarke had a much greater influence, and produced more effect upon the English Army, than all the artillery of the enemy directed against the Duke of York, when commanding in Holland. This lady was remarkable for her beauty and her fascinations, and few came within the circle over which she presided who did not acknowledge her superior power. Her wit, which kept the House of Commons during her examination in a continued state of merriment, was piquant and saucy. Her answers on that occasion have been so often brought before the public, that I need not repeat them, but in private, her quick repartee and her brilliant sallies, rendered her a lively (though not always an agreeable) companion. As for prudence, she had none: her dearest friend – if she had any – was just as likely to be made the object of her ridicule as the most obnoxious person of her acquaintance.

Her narrative of her first introduction to the Duke of York has often been repeated: but as all her stories were considered apocryphal, it is difficult to arrive at a real history of her career. Certain, however, is it that, about the age of sixteen, she was residing at Blackheath – a sweet, pretty, lively girl – when, in her daily walk across the heath, she was passed (on two or three occasions) by a handsome, well-dressed cavalier who, finding that she recognised his salute, dismounted. Pleased with her manner and wit, he begged to be allowed to introduce a friend. Accordingly, on her consenting, a person to whom the cavalier appeared to pay every sort of deference was presented to her, and the acquaintance ripened into something more than friendship.

Not the slightest idea, had the young lady, of the position in society of her lover, until she accompanied him, on his invitation, to the theatre, where she occupied a private box: when she was surprised at the ceremony with which she was treated, and at observing that every eye and every lorgnette in the house were directed towards her in the course of the evening. She accepted this as a tribute to her beauty. Finding that she could go again to the theatre when she pleased and occupy the same box, she availed herself of this opportunity with a female friend, and was not a little astonished at being addressed as Her Royal Highness. She then discovered that the individual into whose affections she had insinuated herself was the Duke of York, son of the king, who had not long before united himself to a lady, for whom she had been mistaken.

Mrs Mary Anne Clarke was soon reconciled to the thought of being the wife of a prince by the left hand, particularly as she found herself assiduously courted by persons of the highest rank, and more especially by military men. A large house in a fashionable street was taken for her[26] and an establishment on a magnificent scale gave her an opportunity of surrounding herself with persons of a sphere far beyond anything she could, in her younger days, have dreamed of: her father having been in an honourable trade and her husband being only a captain in a marching regiment.[27] The duke, delighted to see his fair friend so well received, constantly honoured her dinner table with his presence, and willingly gratified any wish that she expressed, and he must have known (and for this he was afterwards highly censured) that her style of living was upon a scale of great expense and that he himself contributed little towards it. The consequence was that the hospitable lady eventually became embarrassed and knew not which way to turn to meet her outlay. It was suggested to her that she might obtain from the duke commissions in the army, which she could easily dispose of at a good price. Individuals quickly came forward, ready to purchase anything that came within her grasp, which extended not only to the army, but (as it afterwards appeared) to the Church: for there were reverend personages who availed themselves of her assistance and thus obtained patronage, by which they advanced their worldly interests very rapidly.

Amongst those who paid great attention to Mrs Mary Anne Clark was Colonel Wardle, at that time a remarkable member of the House of Commons and a bold leader of the Radical Opposition. He got intimately acquainted with her and was so great a personal favourite that it was believed he wormed out all her secret history, of which he availed himself to obtain a fleeting popularity.

---

26 K. D. Reynold, in the *Oxford Dictionary of National Biography*, states that Clarke 'took a large house in Gloucester Place where she entertained on an extravagant scale, and it was then that rumour first coupled her name with that of the duke.'

27 Reynold's thought that 'In 1791 she is believed to have eloped with Joseph Clarke, son of a builder from Snow Hill; they apparently had two children, though no marriage took place before 1794.'

Having obtained the names of some of the parties who had been fortunate enough – as they imagined – to secure the lady's favour, he loudly demanded an inquiry in the House of Commons as to the management of the army by the commander-in-chief, the Duke of York.[28] The nation and the army were fond of His Royal Highness and every attempt to screen him was made: but in vain. The House undertook the task of investigating the conduct of the duke and witnesses were produced, amongst whom was the fair lady herself, who by no means attempted to screen her imprudent admirer. Her responses to the questions put to her were cleverly and archly given and the whole mystery of her various intrigues came to light.

The duke consequently resigned his place in the Horse Guards and at the same time repudiated the beautiful and dangerous cause of his humiliation. The lady, incensed at the desertion of her royal swain, announced her intention of publishing his love letters, which were likely to expose the whole of the royal family to ridicule, as they formed the frequent themes of his correspondence. Sir Herbert Taylor was therefore commissioned to enter into a negotiation for the purchase of the letters: this he effected at an enormous price,[29] obtaining a written document at the same time, by which Mrs Clarke was subjected to heavy penalties if she, by word or deed, implicated the honour of any of the branches of the royal family. A pension was secured to her, on condition that she should quit England and reside wherever she chose on the Continent. To all this she consented and in the first instance went to Brussels, where her previous history being scarcely known, she was well received, and she married her daughters without any inquiry as to the fathers to whom she might ascribe them.

Mrs Clarke afterwards settled quietly and comfortably in Paris, receiving, occasionally, visits from members of the aristocracy, who had

---

28 Wardle brought eight charges against the duke for misuse of military patronage in 1809. The subsequent investigation failed to prove these, though it was clear Clarke had received payment from individuals for influence over her royal lover. The duke promptly resigned, but returned to his post as commander-in-chief in 1811.

29 Some £7,000 plus a comfortable life annuity.

known her when mingling in a certain circle in London.[30] The Marquis of Londonderry never failed to pay his respects to her, entertaining a very high opinion of her talents. Her manners were exceedingly agreeable and to the latest day, she retained pleasing traces of past beauty. She was lively, sprightly, and full of fun, and indulged in innumerable anecdotes of the members of the royal family of England – some of them much too scandalous to be repeated. She regarded the Duke of York as a big baby, not out of his leading-strings and the Prince of Wales as an idle sensualist with just enough brains to be guided by any laughing, well-bred individual who would listen to his stale jokes and impudent ribaldry. Of Queen Charlotte, she used to speak with the utmost disrespect, attributing to her a love of domination and a hatred of everyone who would not bow down before any idol that she chose to set up, and as being envious of the Princess Caroline and her daughter, the Princess Charlotte of Wales, and jealous of their acquiring too much influence over the Prince of Wales. In short, Mary Anne Clarke had been so intimately let into every secret of the life of the royal family that had she not been tied down, her revelations would have astonished the world, however willing people might have been to believe that they were tinged with scandal and exaggeration.

The way in which Colonel Wardle first obtained information of the sale of commissions was singular enough. He was paying a clandestine visit to Mrs Clarke, when a carriage with the royal livery drove up to the door and the gallant officer was compelled to take refuge under the sofa, but instead of the royal duke, there appeared one of his aides-de-camp, who entered into conversation in so mysterious a manner as to excite the attention of the gentleman under the sofa and led him to believe that the sale of a commission was authorised by the commander-in-chief: though it afterwards appeared that it was a private arrangement of the unwelcome visitor. At the Horse Guards, it had often been suspected there was a mystery connected with commissions that could not be fathomed, as it frequently

---

30 But before decamping for the continent, Clarke spent nine months in prison for libel, after a successful action brought against her by the Right Hon. William Fitzgerald.

happened that the list of promotions agreed on was surreptitiously increased by the addition of new names. This was the crafty handiwork of the accomplished dame: the duke having employed her as his amanuensis and being accustomed to sign her autograph lists without examination.

⤝· 'Romeo' Coates

This singular man, more than forty years ago, occupied a large portion of public attention. His eccentricities were the theme of general wonder and great was the curiosity to catch a glance at as strange a being as any that ever appeared in English society. This extraordinary individual was a native of one of the West India Islands and was represented as a man of extraordinary wealth: to which, however, he had no claim.[31]

About the year 1808, there arrived at the York Hotel, at Bath, a person about the age of fifty, somewhat gentlemanlike, but so different from the usual men of the day that considerable attention was directed to him. He was of good figure but his face was sallow, seamed with wrinkles, and more expressive of cunning than of any other quality. His dress was remarkable: in the daytime he was covered at all seasons with enormous quantities of fur, but the evening costume in which he went to the balls made a great impression from its gaudy appearance: for his buttons, as well as his knee-buckles, were of diamonds. There was, of course, great curiosity to know who this stranger was, and this curiosity was heightened by an announcement that he proposed to appear at the theatre in the character of Romeo.[32] There was something so unlike that impassioned lover in his appearance (so much that indicated a man with few intellectual gifts) that everybody prepared for a failure. No one, however, anticipated the reality.

---

31 Robert Coates (1772–1848) was born in Antigua but the death of his father in 1807 – a wealthy merchant and sugar planter – would leave Coates in possession of an immense fortune.

32 Coates – originally nicknamed 'Diamond Coates' – was a well-known character in Bath. His habit of publicly reciting Shakespeare in a ridiculously affected and overblown manner, attracted the attention of the Theatre Royal, which, on 9th February 1810, put on a production of *Romeo and Juliet* with Coates as Romeo and professional actors taking the other roles.

On the night fixed for his appearance, the house was crowded to suffocation. The playbills had given out that 'an amateur of fashion' would for that night only perform in the character of Romeo. Besides, it was generally whispered that the rehearsals gave indication of comedy rather than tragedy and that his readings were of a perfectly novel character.

The very first appearance of Romeo convulsed the house with laughter. Benvolio prepares the audience for the stealthy visit of the lover to the object of his admiration, and fully did the amateur give expression to one sense of the words uttered, for he was indeed the true representative of a thief stealing onwards in the night, 'With Tarquin's ravishing strides,' and disguising his face as if he were thoroughly ashamed of it. The darkness of the scene did not, however, show his real character so much as the masquerade, when he came forward with a hideous grin and made what he considered his bow, which consisted in thrusting his head forward and bobbing it up and down several times, his body remaining perfectly upright and still, like a toy mandarin with moveable head.

His dress was *outré* in the extreme: whether Spanish, Italian, or English, no one could say. It was like nothing ever worn. In a cloak of sky blue silk, profusely spangled, red pantaloons, a vest of white muslin, surmounted by an enormously thick cravat and a wig *à la* Charles II, capped by an opera hat, he presented one of the most grotesque spectacles ever witnessed upon the stage. The whole of his garments were evidently too tight for him, and his movements appeared so incongruous that every time he raised his arm or moved a limb, it was impossible to refrain from laughter. But what chiefly convulsed the audience was the bursting of a seam in an inexpressible part of his dress, and the sudden extrusion through the red rent of a quantity of white linen sufficient to make a Bourbon flag, which was visible whenever he turned round. This was at first supposed to be a wilful offence against common decency and some disapprobation was evinced; but the utter unconsciousness of the odd creature was soon apparent and then unrestrained mirth reigned throughout the boxes, pit, and gallery. The total want of flexibility of limb, the awkwardness of his gait, and the idiotic manner in which he stood still, all produced a most ludicrous effect: but when his guttural voice was heard and his total misapprehension of every passage in the play – especially the vulgarity of his address to Juliet – were perceived, everyone was satisfied that Shakespeare's Romeo was burlesqued on that occasion.

The balcony scene was interrupted by shrieks of laughter, for in the midst of one of Juliet's impassioned exclamations, Romeo quietly took out his snuff-box and applied a pinch to his nose. On this a wag in the gallery bawled out, 'I say, Romeo, give us a pinch!' When the impassioned lover, in the most affected manner, walked to the side boxes and offered the contents of his box first to the gentlemen and then – with great gallantry – to the ladies. This new interpretation of Shakespeare was hailed with loud bravos, which the actor acknowledged with his usual grin and nod. Romeo then returned to the balcony and was seen to extend his arms, but all passed in dumb show, so incessant were the shouts of laughter. All that went upon the stage was for a time quite inaudible, but previous to the soliloquy, 'I do remember an apothecary,' there was for a moment a dead silence: for in rushed the hero with a precipitate step until he reached the stage lamps, when he commenced his speech in the lowest possible whisper, as if he had something to communicate to the pit that ought not to be generally known, and this tone was kept up throughout the whole of the soliloquy, so that not a sound could be heard.

The amateur actor showed many indications of aberration of mind and seemed rather the object of pity than of amusement. He, however, appeared delighted with himself and also with his audience, for at the conclusion he walked first to the left of the stage and bobbed his head in his usual grotesque manner at the side boxes, then to the right, performing the same feat: after which, going to the centre of the stage with the usual bob and placing his hand upon his left breast, he exclaimed, 'Haven't I done well?' To this inquiry the house, convulsed as it was with shouts of laughter, responded in such a way as delighted the heart of Kean on one great occasion, when he said, 'The pit rose at me.' The whole audience started up as if with one accord, giving a yell of derision, whilst pocket-handkerchiefs waved from all parts of the theatre.

The dying scene was irresistibly comic and I question if Liston, Munden, or Joey Knight, was ever greeted with such merriment: for Romeo dragged the unfortunate Juliet from the tomb, much in the same manner as a washerwoman thrusts into her cart the bag of foul linen. But how shall I describe his death? Out came a dirty silk handkerchief from his pocket, with which he carefully swept the ground, then his opera hat was carefully placed for a pillow and down he laid himself. After various tossings about, he seemed reconciled to the position, but the house vociferously bawled out, 'Die again, Romeo!' and obedient to the command, he rose up and went through the ceremony again. Scarcely had he lain quietly down when the call was again heard and the well-pleased amateur was evidently prepared to enact a third death, but Juliet now rose up from her tomb and gracefully put an end this ludicrous scene by advancing to the front of the stage and aptly applying a quotation from Shakespeare:

'Dying is such sweet sorrow,
That he will die again until tomorrow.'

Thus ended an extravaganza such has seldom been witnessed. For although Coates repeated the play at the Haymarket,[33] amidst shouts of laughter from the playgoers, there never was so ludicrous a performance as that which took place at Bath on the first night of his appearance. Eventually he was driven from the stage with much contumely, in consequence of its having been discovered that, under pretence of acting for a charitable purpose, he had obtained a sum of money for his performances.[34] His love of notoriety led him to have a most singular shell-shaped carriage built in which, drawn by two fine white horses, he was wont to parade in the park. The harness and every available part

---

33 Coates's London debut, at the Haymarket On 9th December 1811, was in the part of Lothario in Nicholas Rowe's The Fair Penitent.

34 Coates always maintained that he performed for charity and referred to himself as 'the Celebrated Philanthropic Amateur'.

of the vehicle (which was really handsome) were blazoned over with his heraldic device – a cock crowing – and his appearance was heralded by the *gamins* of London shrieking out, 'Cock-a-doodle-doo!' Coates eventually quitted London and settled at Boulogne, where a fair lady was induced to become the partner of his existence notwithstanding the ridicule of the whole world.[35]

🐟· Scrope Davies

The name of Scrope Davies[36] is now but little known except in connection with Brummell's exit from the fashionable world of London, yet few men were better received in society or more the fashion than he once was. He was educated at Eton and from thence he migrated in due time to King's College, Cambridge, of which he became a fellow.[37] There he formed those acquaintances that at a later period served as an introduction into that world of which he soon became a distinguished ornament.

His manners and appearance were of the true Brummell type: there was nothing showy in his exterior. He was quiet and reserved in ordinary company but he was the life and soul of those who relished learning and wit, being a ripe scholar and well read, he was always ready with an apt quotation.

---

35 By 1816 Coates's fame had faded and he fell into financial embarrassment, necessitating his retirement to Boulogne. There he met Emma Anne McDowell, whom he married on 6th September 1823, the couple having returned to England. The curtain finally fell on Coates's life when, in 1848, he was crushed between a hansom cab and a private carriage, whilst crossing Russell Street.

36 Scrope Berdmore Davies (1782–1852).

37 Davies entered Eton in September 1794 aged eleven, and according to T. A. J. Burnett, in *The Rise and Fall of a Regency Dandy: the Life and Times of Scrope Berdmore Davies*, 'Eton turned the … clergyman's son into a wit, dandy and a scholar with an entreé into the grandest rooms in London. At the same time it made him into a gambler, a drunkard and a spendthrift who ended his days in ruin.' It was at Cambridge that Davies met Byron, quickly becoming a member of his coterie, and subsequently an intimate friend and gambling partner. 'One of the cleverest men I ever knew in conversation,' according to Byron.

As was the case with many of the foremost men of that day, the greater number of his hours were passed at the gambling-table, where for a length of time he was eminently successful, for he was a first-rate calculator. He seldom played against individuals: he preferred going to the regular establishments. But on one occasion he had, by a remarkable run of good luck, completely ruined a young man who had just reached his majority and come into possession of a considerable fortune. The poor youth sank down upon a sofa in abject misery when he reflected that he was a beggar, for he was on the point of marriage. Scrope Davies, touched by his despair, entered into conversation with him and ended by giving him back the whole of his losses, upon a solemn promise that he never would play again. The only thing that Scrope retained of his winnings was one of the little carriages of that day, called a *dormeuse,* from its being fitted up with a bed, for he said, 'When I travel in it I shall sleep the better for having acted rightly.' The youth kept his promise: but when his benefactor wanted money, he forgot that he owed all he possessed to Scrope's generosity and refused to assist him.

For a long time Scrope Davies was a lucky player but the time arrived when Fortune deserted her old favourite, and shortly after the Dandy dynasty was overthrown, he found himself unable to mingle with the rich, the giddy, and the gay. With the wreck of his fortune – and indeed but little to live upon beyond the amount of his own Cambridge fellowship – he sought repose in Paris, and there, indulging in literary leisure, bade the world farewell.[38]

﹌• The Late Lord Dudley

The English have, as we all know, the reputation among foreigners of being *des origineaux;* and I am inclined to believe that we are a queer race of people and that there are more *characters* among us than are to be found abroad.

---

38 Davies's gambling luck peaked in 1815, but thereafter he lost heavily and by 1819 he was in dire financial straits. In January 1820, Davies decamped to France in order to evade his creditors. Davies died on 24th May 1852 at his Paris lodgings and was buried in the cemetery at Montmartre.

One of the most conspicuous of the eccentric oddities who flourished forty years ago was Lord Dudley.[39] I need not speak of his powers of conversation, which were most brilliant when he chose to exert them, of his sarcastic wit, and cultivated intellect. These great gifts were obscured by a singular absence of mind, which he carried to such a pitch that some persons maintained much of this peculiarity was assumed. Rather an amusing anecdote is related of him, in which the biter was bit: that is, supposing it to have been true that his *distractions* were not altogether genuine.

It happened one day that coming out of the House of Lords, Lord Dudley's carriage was not to be found. It was late at night and Lord Dudley – who, extremely nervous about catching cold – was in a frantic state of excitement. Lord H__ kindly offered to set him down at Dudley House, which proposal was thankfully accepted. During the drive, Lord Dudley began, according to his usual custom, to talk to himself in an audible tone and the burden of his song was as follows: 'A deuce of a bore! This tiresome man has taken me home and will expect me to ask him to dinner. I suppose I must do so but it is a horrid nuisance!'

Lord H__ closed his eyes and assuming the same sleepy, monotonous voice, muttered forth, 'What a dreadful bore! This good-natured fellow Dudley will feel himself obliged to invite me to dinner and I shall be forced to go. I hope he won't ask me, for he gives damned bad dinners.'

Lord Dudley started, looked very much confused, but said nothing. He, however, never forgave his friend: for he prided himself on being a good hater.

Another time, when dining with Lord W__, who particularly piqued himself upon his dinners, he began apologising to the company for the badness of the *entrées,* and excused himself for their execrable quality on account of the illness of his cook.

---

39 John William Ward, earl of Dudley (1781–1833), politician and foreign secretary under the Canning, Goderich, and Wellington Ministries, who later suffered from bizarre eccentricities of behaviour, including a peculiar habit of holding conversations with himself in several voices.

He was once paying a morning visit to the beautiful Lady M__. He sat an unconscionably long time and the lady, after giving him some friendly hints, took up her work and tried to make conversation. Lord Dudley broke a long fit of silence by muttering, 'A very pretty woman this Lady M__! She stays a devilish long time, I wish she'd go!' He thought Lady M__ was paying him a visit in his own house.[40]

🐀· Captain Hesse

One of my most intimate friends was the late Captain Hesse, generally believed to be the son of the Duke of York by a German lady of rank. Though it is not my intention to disclose certain family secrets of which I am in possession, I may, nevertheless, record some circumstances connected with the life of my friend, which were familiar to a large circle with whom I mixed.

Hesse, in early youth, lived with the Duke and Duchess of York. He was treated in such a manner by them as to indicate an interest in him by their Royal Highnesses that could scarcely be attributed to ordinary regard; and was gazetted a cornet in the 18th Hussars at seventeen years of age. Shortly afterwards he went to Spain and was present in all the battles in which his regiment was engaged, receiving a severe wound in the wrist at the battle of Vittoria. When this became known in England a royal lady wrote to Lord Wellington, requesting that he might be carefully attended to, and at the same time a watch with her portrait was forwarded, which was delivered to the wounded hussar by Lord Wellington himself. When he had sufficiently recovered, Hesse returned to England and passed much of his time at Oatlands, the residence of the Duchess of York. He was also honoured with the confidence of the Princess Charlotte and her mother, Queen Caroline.

---

40 By 1832 Dudley was showing increasing signs of derangement and was subsequently placed under restraint. He never appeared in public again and died on 6th March 1833 after suffering several strokes. Fellow Parliamentarian, Thomas Creevey, summed up Dudley's life thus: 'Poor Ward, with all his acquirements and talents, made little of it, went mad and died.'

Many delicate and important transactions were conducted through the medium of Captain Hesse. In fact, it was perfectly well known that he played a striking part in many scenes of domestic life, which I do not wish to reveal. I may, however, observe that the Prince Regent sent the late Admiral Lord Keith to Hesse's lodgings, who demanded, in His Royal Highness' name, the restitution of the watch and letters that had been sent him when in Spain. After a considerable amount of hesitation, the Admiral obtained what he wanted on the following day, whereupon Lord Keith assured him that the Prince Regent would never forget so great a mark of confidence and that the heir to the throne would ever afterwards be his friend. I regret to say, from personal knowledge, that upon this occasion the prince behaved most ungratefully and unfeelingly: for, after having obtained all he wanted, he positively refused to receive Hesse at Carlton House.

Hesse's life was full of singular incidents. He was a great friend of the Queen of Naples, grandmother of the ex-sovereign of the Two Sicilies. In fact, so notorious was that *liaison,* that Hesse was eventually expelled from Naples under an escort of *gendarmes.* He was engaged in several affairs of honour, in which he always displayed the utmost courage, and his romantic career terminated by his being killed in a duel by Count Léon, natural son of the first Napoleon.[41] He died as he had lived, beloved by his friends and leaving behind him little but his name and the kind thoughts of those who survived him.

🦌· Lord Jersey And An Officer Of The Guards

When duelling was at its height in England, the most absurd pretexts were made for calling a man out. I recollect that at one of the dinners at the Thatched House in St James's Street, Mr Willis, the proprietor, in passing behind the chairs occupied by the company, was accosted by a captain in the 3rd Guards in a rather satirical manner. Mr Willis,

---

41 Charles-Léon Denuelle (1806–81), known as 'comte Léon' was a notorious spendthrift and gambler, and an illegitimate son of Napoleon, by Eléonore Denuelle de la Plaigne.

smarting under the caustic remarks of the gallant captain said aloud, 'Sir, I wrote to you at the request of Lady Jersey, saying that as her Ladyship was unacquainted with you, I had been instructed to reply to your letter by stating that the Lady Patronesses declined sending you a ticket for the ball.' This statement, made in a public room, greatly irritated the captain – his friends in vain endeavoured to calm his wrath – and he sent a cartel the following day to Lord Jersey, requesting he would name his seconds etc. Lord Jersey replied in a very dignified manner, saying that if all persons who did not receive tickets from his wife were to call him out for want of courtesy on her part, he should have to make up his mind to become a target for young officers, and he therefore declined the honour of the proposed meeting.

๛• Colonel Kelly And His Blacking

Among the odd characters I have met with, I do not recollect anyone more eccentric than the late Lieutenant Colonel Kelly of the 1st Foot Guards, who was the vainest man I ever encountered. He was a thin and emaciated-looking dandy but had all the bearing of a gentleman. He was haughty in the extreme and very fond of dress. His boots were so well varnished that the polish now in use could not surpass Kelly's blacking in brilliancy; his pantaloons were made of the finest leather and his coats were inimitable: in short, his dress was considered perfect.

His sister held the place of housekeeper to the Customhouse and when it was burnt down, Kelly was burnt with it, in endeavouring to save his favourite boots. When the news of this horrible death became known, all the dandies were anxious to secure the services of his valet, who possessed the mystery of the inimitable blacking. Brummell lost no time in discovering his place of residence and asked what wages he required. The servant answered that his late master gave him £150 a year but it was not enough for his talents and he should require £200. Upon which, Brummell said: 'Well, if you will make it guineas, *I* shall be happy to attend upon *you*.' The late Lord Plymouth eventually secured this phoenix of valets at £200 a year and bore away the sovereignty of boots.

🦢· Mr Lawrence, The Celebrated Surgeon

It was my good fortune to have known Mr Lawrence, who was allowed to have been the most scientific, as well as one of the most skilful surgeons England or Europe could boast of at that time. The opinion entertained of him by the faculty was evinced by the many high encomiums passed upon his talents by his contemporaries. He was the most accomplished and gentlest of mankind, and ever ready to render the slightest service to a friend in distress.[42]

Upon one occasion I called upon him at his house in Whitehall, opposite the Admiralty, and told him that half an hour before I had seen a pretty girl, an opera dancer, unable to move from her sofa owing to 'soft corns', which precluded her from appearing on the stage. 'Bring her here, my friend Gronow, and I will endeavour to cure her, but do not mention to anyone that I have turned chiropodist.' I lost no time in calling upon the *danseuse*, and prevailed upon her to place herself under the care of my skilful friend.

Some few days elapsed, when I met Lawrence in his carriage and was invited by him to take a drive, during which he asked me if I had seen the young lady, whom he had operated upon and completely cured. Upon my replying in the negative, he said, 'It is always so when you render a service to persons possessing neither principle nor feeling; you are sure to be treated with ingratitude.' This lady became immensely rich, and I regret to add that the surgeon's fee was never paid, which I had good reason to know amounted to twenty guineas ...

🦢· Colonel Mackinnon

Commonly called 'Dan', Colonel Mackinnon[43] was an exceedingly well-made man and remarkable for his physical powers in running, jumping,

---

42 In 1815 Sir William Lawrence was a professor of anatomy and physiology at the Royal College of Surgeons, where he was destined to receive many honours from the medical establishment. He was appointed sergeant-surgeon to Queen Victoria in 1857.
43 Daniel Mackinnon (1791–1836).

climbing, and such bodily exercises as demanded agility and muscular strength. He used to amuse his friends by creeping over the furniture of a room like a monkey. It was very common for his companions to make bets with him: for example, that he would not be able to climb up the ceiling of a room, or scramble over a certain house-top. Grimaldi, the famous clown, used to say, 'Colonel Mackinnon has only to put on the motley costume and he would totally eclipse me!'

Mackinnon was famous for practical jokes, which were, however, always played in a gentlemanly way. Before landing at St Andero's with some other officers who had been on leave in England, he agreed to impersonate the Duke of York and make the Spaniards believe that His Royal Highness was amongst them. On nearing the shore, a royal standard was hoisted at the masthead and Mackinnon disembarked, wearing the star of his shako on his left breast and accompanied by his friends, who agreed to play the part of aide-de-camp to royalty. The Spanish authorities were soon informed of the arrival of the royal commander-in-chief of the British Army: so they received Mackinnon with the usual pomp and circumstance attending such occasions. The mayor of the place, in honour of the illustrious arrival, gave a grand banquet, which terminated with the appearance of a huge bowl of punch. Whereupon Dan, thinking that the joke had gone far enough, suddenly dived his head into the porcelain vase and threw his heels into the air. The surprise and indignation of the solemn Spaniards were such that they made a most intemperate report of the hoax to Lord Wellington. Dan, however, was ultimately forgiven after a severe reprimand.

Another of his freaks very nearly brought him to a court martial. Lord Wellington was curious about visiting a convent near Lisbon and the Lady Abbess made no difficulty. Mackinnon, hearing this, contrived to get clandestinely within the sacred walls, and it was generally supposed that it was neither his first nor his second visit. At all events, when Lord Wellington arrived, Dan Mackinnon was to be seen among the nuns, dressed out in their sacred costume, with his head and whiskers shaved, and as he possessed good features, he was declared to be one of the best-looking amongst those chaste dames.[44] It was supposed that this adventure, which was known to Lord Byron, suggested a similar episode in *Don Juan*, the scene being laid in the East. I might say more about Dan's adventures in the convent but have no wish to be scandalous …

🦎· Mr Neeld

Lord Alvanley having been invited to dine in Grosvenor Square, at the house of Mr Neeld – the heir to Mr Rundell, the wealthy goldsmith – was, previous to sitting down to table, shown some fine pictures, which hung on the walls of the drawing-room; together with many articles of *virtù* that crowded the apartment. The host praising and describing each – and stating the cost in by no means a well-bred manner. One would have thought that the infliction would have been discontinued on entering the dining-room, but on the guests being seated, Mr Neeld began excusing himself for not having a haunch of venison for dinner and assured his guests that a very fine haunch of Welsh mutton had been prepared for them. He then returned to his favourite topic and began praising the room in which they were dining and the furniture. He had got to the gilding, which he assured his guests had been done by French artists at an enormous expense, when the mutton made its appearance. Lord Alvanley, who been intensely bored, exclaimed: 'I care not what your gilding cost but what is more to the purpose, I am most anxious to make a trial of your *carving*, Mr Neeld, for I am excessively hungry and should like to attack the representative of the haunch of venison.'

The *nouveau riche*, though rather astonished by this remark, was obliged to let it pass without notice: his anxiety to form a circle of aristocratic acquaintances preventing his taking offence at anything said by such a person as his Lordship.

---

44 According to Stanhope, in *Conversations with Wellington*, the duke himself told a version of Mackinnon's stunt at the convent, in which, having been invited into the parlour to hear the nuns sing, the whole party was 'amazed at seeing one of the nuns, as it seemed, suddenly turn head over heels, and her petticoats falling about her head, display the boots and trousers of an officer!'

⇜• Kate North

In the days when 'Skittles',[45] 'Anonyma',[46] and other descendants of the
Laises and Phrynes[47] of old are topics of conversation and newspaper
comment, I may be permitted to 'point a moral and adorn a tale' by relating
a remarkable episode in the life and adventures of the beautiful – and once
celebrated – Kate North.

Kate was the daughter of a discharged sergeant of the Guards, who
had the appointment of sutler at Chatham. Her mother dying after a long
illness, Kate, though young, worked hard early and late and managed her
father's house for a length of time – and the entire garrison, from the
commanding officer to the private soldier, were loud in their praise of
this incomparable young girl, whose marvellous beauty was the theme
of conversation.

Among the officers at Chatham there happened to be a young ensign,
extremely good-looking, upon whom Kate's beauty made a strong
impression. He succeeded in captivating the affections of the charming
and innocent girl and at last seduced her. The regiment to which the ensign
belonged having received marching orders, Kate determined to follow her
seducer and she marched with the soldiers to London. The secret of her
seduction was not long before it got known and reached the ears of the
commander-in-chief, the Duke of York,[48] who, being informed that the
poor girl was in a state of destitution, sent an aide-de-camp to discover
her retreat, which proved to be an unfurnished room in the worst part of
Spitalfields. The aide-de-camp told her his errand but at the same time
bound her to secrecy.

Early robbed of her virtue, abandoned by her betrayer, and an utter
stranger in London, she reproached herself with her sin and in a paroxysm
of remorse and despair, the wretched girl determined to poison herself. She

---

45 The pet name of Catherine Walters, the internationally-renowned courtesan.
46 The nom de plume of a contemporary 'kiss-and-tell' scandal-monger.
47 References to courtesans of the Classical Age, the latter being the statuesque model
   and mistress of the Ancient Greek sculptor, Praxiteles.
48 Field Marshal Frederick Augustus (1763–1827), second son of George III.

had purchased some laudanum[49] and was on the point of swallowing it, when a gentle rap at the door was heard. She opened the door and in walked the Duke of York. His Royal Highness was struck with her beauty, modest deportment, and the frankness with which she answered all his questions, and on taking his leave, said that he would send her a few necessaries to make her comfortable. Upon which, the poor girl fell upon her knees and in a voice almost inarticulate with emotion, thanked her benefactor.

When the duke again called, she expressed her gratitude for all she had received but hinted to her royal visitor that her earnest desire was to live an honourable life. The duke was astounded but said nothing in reply. He was simply dressed in a plain riding costume and was, without exception, one of the finest men England could boast of. He stood above six feet, was rather stout (but well-proportioned), his chest broad and his frame muscular. His face bore the stamp of authority and every feature was handsome: his brow was full and prominent, the eye greyish, beaming with benevolence, and a noble forehead with premature grey hairs – though the prince was hardly in the vale of years – completed the picture, which presented itself to the unhappy Kate. The poor girl, overawed by the royal presence, attempted to leave the room but was prevented. Her thoughts were how to avoid the danger that she felt was awaiting her, if the royal duke should persist in his assiduities.

His Royal Highness, not knowing the girl's feelings, paid her frequent visits and each succeeding day became more and more enamoured of her: though upon all occasions she evinced a desire to avoid his presence. The thoughts of her seducer and the degrading situation in which she stood, contrasting with the benevolence and apparent affection of the royal duke, overwhelmed her. She wept bitterly and flung herself upon her bed in an agony of distress. Her first resolution was to tell the duke that she could not bring herself to consent to his proposals, but scarcely was the resolution

---

49 An alcoholic beverage made from opium and containing morphine, which was prescribed as a general pain-killer and tonic. Its use – and abuse – was widespread, especially since, as a medicinal drug, it was not taxed and therefore cheaper than wine or spirit.

formed, when the royal visitor again made his appearance. He promised never to desert her and at length, overcome by his kindness and his importunities, she exclaimed: 'If you really love me, duke, I consent to be yours.' The duke was made happy: a house, carriages, etc., were supplied to the fair Kate, who lived with him many years. As she had a love for reading and a desire for knowledge, masters were engaged for her, and by dint of perseverance and applying herself to study, she was enabled to dissipate that weight of sorrow, which would have otherwise hastened her death.

One summer morning a friend of the Duke of York's called and told her that His Royal Highness would be under the necessity of giving up his connection with her, for he had promised the king, his father, that if his debts were paid, he would never more see the object of his affection. Poor Kate's heart was full. She could not reply to the messenger but bursting into tears, hid her face, and flew out of the room. The sting that had been inflicted was more than she could bear and she was seized with brain fever: but with much care and quiet, in course of time, the poor creature recovered her health and composure of mind.

There was no woman so much admired in London at the time as Kate North. Her bewitching manners, the charm and grace of her conversation, brought to her pretty house in Green Street innumerable admirers. Among those anxious to woo her, a noble Scotch lord was most assiduous in his attentions, and he at length succeeded in prevailing upon her to accept the offer of his protection. She lived with him several years and bore him a daughter, who is now the wife of a baronet and the mother of a numerous family. But the canker in Kate's mind was corroding her life. She visited Paris for change of air and scene, but there her senses left her: she became raving mad and died in a foreign land, without a friend to close her eyes.

☞· Count D'Orsay

In speaking of this gifted and accomplished man,[50] I shall strictly confine myself – as I have done in other instances – to his public character, and

---

50 Gédéon Gaspard Alfred de Grimaud, Count D'Orsay (1801–1852) artist and sculptor.

not enter into the details of his private life: which are, perhaps, better left in the shade.[51] I first saw him at an evening party given in 1816 by his grandmother, the well-known Madame Crawford, in the Rue d'Anjou Saint Honoré. He was then sixteen years old and he appeared to be a general favourite, owing to his remarkable beauty and pleasing manners. His father and mother were both present and did me the honour to invite me to their house in the Rue Mount Blanc (now called the Rue de la Chausée d'Antin). They occupied the apartment in which the celebrated composer Rossini now lives. D'Orsay's father, justly surnamed Le Beau D'Orsay, was one of the handsomest men in the French Army: one of Napoleon's generals, he distinguished himself in Spain, particularly at the battle of Salamanca.[52]

I believe (and I like to think) that had Count D'Orsay fallen into good hands, he might have been a great many things that he was not. Unfortunate circumstances, which entangled him as with a fatal web from his early youth, dragged him downwards and led him step by step to his ruin. On these peculiar circumstances I shall not dwell. They are known to all and cannot be palliated. But he was a grand creature in spite of all this: beautiful as the Apollo Belvidere in his outward form, full of health, life, spirits, wit and gaiety. Such was Count D'Orsay when I first knew him. If the Count had been born with a fortune of £100,000 a year, he would have been a great man. He loved money – not for money's sake but for what it could procure. He was generous even to ostentation and he had a real pleasure in giving even what he himself had borrowed. He was born with princely tastes and ideas and would have heartily despised a man who could have sat down contented in a simple dwelling place with a bad cook and a small competence.[53]

---

51 A reference, no doubt, to D'Orsay's scandalous ménage à trois – with Lord and Lady Blessington, which was common knowledge at the time, and had the effect of excluding from the Frenchman's society any persons of moral standing or good character.

52 Wellington's victory over Marshal Marmont on 22nd July 1812.

53 D'Orsay was notoriously vain, selfish, and irresponsible with money, spending vast sums he simply did not possess on clothes, carriages, gambling, etc. Most of his debts were settled by Lady Blessington, and when, in 1849, D'Orsay was obliged to escape his creditors by fleeing to France, she sold all her possessions to join him.

He possessed in a great degree the faculty of pleasing those whom he wished to attract. His smile was bright and genial, his manner full of charm, his conversation original and amusing, and his artistic taste undeniable. It might have been objected that this taste was somewhat too gaudy: but the brilliant tints with which he liked to surround himself suited his style of beauty, dress, and manner. When I used to see him driving in his tilbury some thirty years ago, I fancied that he looked like some gorgeous dragon-fly skimming through the air: and though all was dazzling and showy, yet there was a kind of harmony, which precluded any idea or accusation of bad taste. All his imitators fell between the Scylla and Charybdis of tigerism and charlatanism: but he escaped those quicksands – though perhaps somewhat narrowly – in spite of a gaudy and almost eccentric style of dress.

Many of his *bon-mots* and clever sayings have been cited by his numerous friends and admirers, but perhaps there was more humour and *à propos* in the majority of them than actual wit. There was also much in his charming manner and the very successful mixture of French and English that he had adopted in conversation. I call to mind a story of him not generally known. When he first came to England as a very young man, and was about twenty-two years of age, he was invited to dine at Holland House, where he was seated next to Lady Holland herself, who supposed that the handsome stranger was a shy young man, awe-struck by her majestic selfishness. Owing to a considerable abdominal development, her ladyship was continually letting her napkin slip from her lap to the ground, and as often as she did so, she smiled blandly but authoritatively on the French count, and asked him to pick it up. He politely complied several times, but at last tired of this exercise, he said, to her great surprise, 'Ne ferais-je pas mieux, Madame, de m'asseoir sous la table, afin de pouvoir vous passer la serviette plus rapidement?' [54]

On another occasion, the well-known Tom Raikes, whose letters and memoirs have been lately published, and who was a tall, large man, very

---

54 'I should, Madam, perhaps do better to sit under the table, in order to pass the napkin more quickly to you.'

much marked with the smallpox, having one day written an anonymous letter to D'Orsay, containing some piece of impertinence or other, had closed it with a wafer and stamped it with something resembling the top of a thimble. The count soon discovered who was the writer and in a room full of company thus addressed him: 'Ha, ha! My good Raikes, the next time you write an anonymous letter, you must not seal it with your nose!'

I cannot conclude without giving some description of the personal appearance of one who reigned pre-eminent in the fashionable circles of London and Paris. He was rather above six feet in height and when I first knew him, he might have served as a model for a statuary. His neck was long, his shoulders broad, and his waist narrow, and though he was, perhaps, somewhat underlimbed, nothing could surpass the beauty of his feet and ankles. His dark chestnut hair hung naturally in long waving curls, his forehead was high and wide, his features regular, and his complexion glowed with radiant health. His eyes were large and of a light hazel colour. He had full lips and very white teeth but a little apart, which sometimes gave to the generally amiable expression of his countenance a rather cruel and sneering look, such as one sees in the heads of some of the old Roman emperors. He was wonderfully strong and active and excelled in manly exercises. He was a fine horseman, a good swordsman, and a fair shot. I knew him intimately and saw a great deal of him. He had an amusing *naïveté* in speaking of his own personal advantages.

I remember on one occasion, when about to fight a duel, he said to his second, Monsieur D__, who was making the preliminary arrangements, 'You know, my dear friend, I am not on a par with my antagonist: he is a very ugly fellow and if I wound him in the face, he won't look much the worse for it, but on my side it ought to be agreed that he should not aim higher than my chest, for if my face should be spoiled, *'ce serait vraiment dommage.'* He said this with such a beaming smile and looked so handsome and happy, that his friend, Monsieur D__, fully agreed with him.

Though his tastes, pursuits, and habits were thoroughly manly, yet he took as much care of his beauty as a woman might have done. He was in the habit of taking perfumed baths and his friends remember the enormous gold dressing-case, which it required two men to carry, and which used to be the companion of all his excursions. Peace be to his ashes! It will be long before the world looks upon his like again.[55]

⨠ Lord Petersham And Harrington House

When our army returned to England in 1814, my young friend Augustus Stanhope took me one afternoon to Harrington House, in Stableyard, St James's, where I was introduced to Lord and Lady Harrington and all the Stanhopes. On entering a long gallery, I found the whole family engaged in their sempiternal occupation of tea-drinking. Neither in Nanking, Peking, nor Canton was the teapot more assiduously and constantly replenished than at this hospitable mansion. I was made free of the corporation, if I may use the phrase, by a cup being handed to me, and I must say that I never tasted any tea so good before or since.

As an example of the undeviating tea-table habits of the house of Harrington, General Lincoln Stanhope once told me, after an absence of several years in India, he made his reappearance at Harrington House and found the family, as he had left them on his departure, drinking tea in the long gallery. On his presenting himself, his father's only observation and speech of welcome to him was, 'Hallo Linky, my dear boy! Delighted to see you. Have a cup of tea?'

I was then taken to Lord Petersham's apartments,[56] where we found his Lordship – one of the chief dandies of the day – employed in making a particular sort of blacking, which he said would eventually supercede every other. The room into which we were ushered was more like a shop than a gentleman's sitting-room: all around the walls were shelves, upon which were placed tea-canisters containing Congou, Pekoe, Souchong, Bohea, Gunpowder, Russian, and many other teas, all the best of their kind; on the other side of the room were beautiful jars with names, in

---

55 D'Orsay died on 4th August 1852 following a spinal infection. He was buried alongside Lady Blessington, who had died shortly after joining him in Paris, in a stone pyramid, which he had designed for her and had constructed at Chambourcy.

56 Charles Stanhope (1780–1851) succeeded as fourth earl of Harrington in 1829.

gilt letters, of innumerable kinds of snuff and all the necessary apparatus for moistening and mixing. Lord Petersham's mixture is still well-known to all tobacconists. Other shelves and many of the tables were covered with a great number of magnificent snuff-boxes: for Lord Petersham had perhaps the finest collection in England and was supposed to have a fresh box for every day in the year. I heard him, on the occasion of a delightful old light-blue Sèvres box he was using being admired, say in his lisping way, 'Yes, it is a nice summer box but would not do for winter wear.'

In this museum there were also innumerable canes of very great value. The Viscount was likewise a great Mæcenas among the tailors and a particular kind of greatcoat, when I was a young man, was called a petersham.[57]

In person, Lord Petersham was tall and handsome and possessed of a particularly winning smile. He very much resembled the pictures of Henry IV of France and frequently wore a dress not unlike that of the celebrated monarch. His carriages were unique of their kind: they were entirely brown with brown horses and harness. The groom, a tall youth, was dressed in a long brown coat reaching to his heels and a glazed hat with a large cockade. It is said that Lord Petersham's devotion to brown was caused by his having been desperately in love with a very beautiful widow bearing that name.[58]

In addition to his other eccentricities, Lord Petersham never ventured out of doors till six p.m. His manners were decidedly affected and he spoke with a kind of lisp. But in spite of his little foibles, Lord Petersham was a thorough gentleman and was beloved by all who knew him.

---

57 According to K. D. Reynolds, in the *Oxford Dictionary of National Biography*, 'He was a great dandy, affecting the immaculate dress, exaggerated manners, and eccentricities of behaviour of his kind, and featured frequently in contemporary prints. He wore distinctive hats, designed the overcoat that became known as the petersham, was a connoisseur of both tea and snuff, and pursued women with more drama than discretion.'

58 According to Countess Lieven, Mrs Brown was not a widow, and when her husband discovered Petersham's advances he gave him a public thrashing.

➤ Raggett, Of White's Club

Raggett, the well known club proprietor of White's, and the Roxburgh Club in St James's Square, was a notable character in his way. He began life as a poor man, and died extremely rich. It was his custom to wait upon the members of these clubs whenever play was going on. Upon one occasion at the Roxburgh, the following gentlemen, Hervey Combe, Typo Smith, Ward (the Member for London) and Sir John Malcolm, played at high stakes at whist: they sat during that night, viz., Monday, the following day and night, and only separated on Wednesday morning at eleven o'clock. Indeed, the party only broke up then owing to Hervey Combe being obliged to attend the funeral of one of his partners who was buried on that day. Hervey Combe, on looking over his card, found that he was a winner of £30,000 from Sir John Malcolm, and he jocularly said, 'Well, Sir John, you shall have your revenge whenever you like.' Sir John replied, 'Thank you, another sitting of the kind will oblige me to return again to India.' Hervey Combe, on settling with Raggett, pulled out of his pocket a handful of counters, which amounted to several hundred pounds, over and above the 30,000 he had won of the baronet, and he gave them to Raggett, saying, 'I give them to you for sitting so long with us, and providing us with all required.' Raggett was overjoyed, and in mentioning what had occurred to one of his friends a few days afterwards, he added, 'I make it a rule never to allow any of my servants to be present when gentlemen play at my clubs, for it is my invariable custom to sweep the carpet after the gambling is over, and I generally find on the floor a few counters, which pays me for the trouble of sitting up. By this means I have made a decent fortune.'[59]

59 White's Club, at 37–38 St James's Street, was the oldest and most prestigious of the St James's gentlemen's clubs. George Raggett took over as proprietor in 1812, one year after the club's famous bow window – so beloved by Brummell – was added. At this time the club had a membership of some 500 persons, with a substantial waiting list for prospective members.

⟩⟨· Shelley

Shelley[60] the poet, cut off at so early an age, just when his great poetical talents had been matured by study and reflection, was my friend and associate at Eton. He was a boy of studious and meditative habits, averse to all games and sports and a great reader of novels and romances. He was a thin, slight lad, with remarkably lustrous eyes, fine hair, and a very peculiar shrill voice and laugh. His most intimate friend at Eton was a boy named Price, who was considered one of the best classical scholars amongst us. At his tutor, Bethell's, where he lodged, he attempted many mechanical and scientific experiments. By the aid of a common tinker, he contrived to make something like a steam engine, which unfortunately, one day, suddenly exploded to the great consternation of the neighbourhood and to the imminent danger of a severe flogging from Dr Goodall.[61]

Soon after leaving school, about the year 1810, he came in a state of great distress and difficulty to Swansea, when we had an opportunity of rendering him a service, but we never could ascertain what had brought him to Wales (though we had reason to suppose it was some mysterious *affaire du cœur*).[62]

The last time I saw Shelley was at Genoa in 1822,[63] sitting on the seashore, and when I came upon him (making a true poet's meal of bread and fruit) he at once recognised me, jumped up, and appearing greatly delighted, exclaimed: 'Here you see me at my old Eton habits, but instead of the green fields for a couch, I have here the shores of the Mediterranean. It is very grand and very romantic. I only wish I had some of the excellent

---

60 Percy Bysshe Shelley (1792–1822).

61 Joseph Goodall – generally accepted to have been a jovial figure – was headmaster at Eton between 1801-09, when he was replaced by his former assistant, the notorious disciplinarian, John Keate.

62 By 1811 Shelley was a troubled man indeed: a declaration of atheism had resulted in his expulsion from Oxford University and a breakdown in relations with his father. Shelley's elopement and marriage to Harriet Westbrook, the sixteen-year-old daughter of a coffee house owner, only made matters worse, and his father cut off his allowance and refused to communicate with him.

63 Shelley had left England for Italy in 1818, because of financial and health problems.

brown bread and butter we used to get at Spier's. But I never was very fastidious in my diet.' Then he continued in a wild and eccentric manner: 'Gronow, do you remember the beautiful Martha, the Hebe of Spier's?[64] She was the loveliest girl I ever saw and I loved her to distraction.'

Shelley was looking careworn and ill, and as usual was very carelessly dressed. He had on a large and wide straw hat, his long brown hair, already streaked with grey, flowing in large masses from under it, and presented a wild and strange appearance.

During the time I sat by his side he asked many questions about myself and many of our school-fellows. But on my questioning him in turn about himself, his way of life, and his future plans, he avoided entering into any explanation. Indeed, he gave such short and evasive answers that, thinking my inquisitiveness displeased him, I rose to take my leave. I observed that I had not been lucky enough to see Lord Byron in any of my rambles, to which he replied, 'Byron is living in his villa, surrounded by his court of sycophants, but I shall shortly see him at Leghorn.' We then shook hands. I never saw him again, for he was drowned shortly afterwards with his friend, Captain Williams, and his body was washed ashore near Viareggio. Everyone is familiar with the romantic scene that took place on the seashore, when the remains of my poor friend and Captain Williams were burnt, in the presence of Byron and Trelawny, in the Roman fashion. His ashes were gathered into an urn and buried in the Protestant cemetery at Rome. He was but twenty-nine years of age at his death.[65]

⩯• Admiral Sir Richard Strachan

This brave sailor[66] was famous for many daring actions and gallant feats of arms, but will perhaps be best known to posterity by the celebrated

---

64 In Greek mythology, Hebe was the goddess of youth.

65 On 8th July 1822, Shelley's boat, the *Don Juan* accidentally sank in bad weather: the poet and his friend, Captain Williams were drowned, Shelley's body being washed ashore ten days later. Originally buried on the beach, the bodies of Shelley and Williams were exhumed on 16th August and cremated near Viareggio.

66 Sir Richard John Strachan, fourth baronet (1760–1828).

verses on the Walcheren expedition:[67]

> *Sir Richard, longing to be at 'em,*
> *Was waiting for the Earl of Chatham;*
> *The earl of Chatham, all forlorn,*
> *Was waiting for Sir Richard Strachan!*

In the piping times of peace, when there was no longer any hostile fleet to watch or stray French squadron to capture, the veteran turned his whole attention to the worship and admiration of the fair sex, and displayed the same ardour in the pursuit of a pretty girl or handsome matron as he had formerly shown in the chase of a fine frigate or tight little schooner.[68] His field of action, which had once been the Channel, the North Sea, or the Mediterranean, was now confined to Bond Street, Piccadilly, or the squares and parks. He always rode a grey horse, and the 'Old Admiral' was as well-known to the Londoners of his day as the Iron Duke was to everyone in town some twenty or thirty years ago.

In his sixty-first year,[69] Sir Richard fell desperately in love with a young girl – daughter of a man who kept a china shop in South Audley Street – and though married and the father of a large family, he persecuted this beauty with his attentions from morning till night. He would pass and repass the house where her father lived at least 100 times a day, and send her gigantic bouquets and presents without number.

These proceedings created much scandal in the neighbourhood, and the father of the girl was determined to put a stop to the admiral's wicked design to run off with his daughter.

---

67 The ill-fated British invasion of this Dutch island, under Lord Chatham, between August and September 1809, achieved nothing – except the temporary seizure of the port of Flushing – and at a cost of 106 men killed in action and 4,000 killed by malaria or 'Walcheren Fever'.

68 In 1810, having been made a scapegoat for the failure of Chatham's expedition, Strachan – or 'Mad Dick' was he was known to his men, on account of his violent temper – was promoted to vice-admiral, marrying Louisa Dillon two years later.

69 i.e. 1821, the year Strachan was promoted from vice-admiral to full admiral.

It had been proposed by Sir Richard to the fair Sophy R__ that she was to meet him at 9 p.m. opposite Fladong's Hotel, where a carriage and four would be in readiness. She appeared to agree to this proposal, but the admiral, on arriving at the place of rendezvous, found, instead of the girl, her father and brother armed with bludgeons, with which they belaboured him to their hearts' content. The old *Lovelace* defended himself as best he could till the watchmen in the neighbourhood came to the rescue and took all parties to Marlborough Street, where they remained in durance vile [prison] during the night.

The following morning they were brought before the magistrate, who was proceeding to interrogate them, when Admiral Lord Gardner entered to swear an affidavit, and perceiving Sir Richard in a miserable plight and surrounded by a motley crowd, exclaimed in true melodramatic style: 'What do I see! Dicky Strachan a prisoner and his colours struck! Impossible! Impossible!'

The magistrate begged an explanation of what had occurred on the previous night, when Sir Richard stated that he had been attacked and severely beaten by two men with bludgeons: but he refused to swear that the persons present were the culprits, for the night was dark, and he could not identify them. In short, though he had been so badly treated, the gallant veteran would not say a word against the father and brother of his beloved Sophy. The father, however, carried his point, for the admiral ceased cruising in the *china* seas and the gallant grey and his rider were never again seen in the neighbourhood of South Audley Street.

✒· General Thornton and Theodore Hook

On the return of the British Army from Spain in 1814, the Prince Regent, desirous of rewarding the personal associates of the Duke of Wellington, decided on removing the generals of the Guards and giving their places to officers of the duke's staff who ranked as colonels. The generals were mostly either useless and decrepit veterans or officers whose ideas of service consisted in attending as little as possible to their regiments and giving the balance of their time to pleasure.

One of them, General Thornton, was afflicted with the idea that of all persons in the world he was the only one who understood the art of waltzing. In fact, it was quite a mania with him and he might be seen at nearly every party of note, making himself exceedingly ridiculous by teaching young ladies to waltz – this dance having only shortly before come into fashion. Theodore Hook[70] gave him the sobriquet of the Waltzing General – this occasioned a violent altercation between them at a ball in Portman Square, where, it is said, the general received a more personal affront from Hook, which, however, the soldier did not resent according to the then received notions of honour, by calling him out.

The inquiry into this affair by a committee of the other officers of the Guards, no doubt caused the sweeping change proposed by the Prince Regent: it was found that General Thornton had been guilty of cowardice in not demanding immediate satisfaction of Hook, and he was therefore desired to quit the regiment forthwith. His resignation and the comments on it at the time, paved the way to changes in command, and when Hook heard that the companies had been given to the duke's colonels, he said: 'I rejoice to hear that they have adopted Wellington's *overalls* and discarded their *inexpressibles*. These colonels were ever after called the Wellington Overalls.

🐾· Townsend The Bow Street Officer

Townsend, the famous Bow Street officer,[71] when I knew him, was a little fat man with a flaxen wig, kerseymere breeches, a blue straight-cut coat, and a broad-brimmed hat. To the most daring courage he added great dexterity and cunning, and was said, *in propriâ personâ*, to have taken more thieves than all the other Bow Street officers put together. He frequently accompanied mail coaches when the government required large sums of money to be conveyed to distant parts of the country.[72]

---

70 Theodore Edward Hook (1788–1841), writer and notorious practical joker.

71 John Townsend (1760–1832).

72 Appointed an officer of the court in 1781, Townsend was authorised to make criminal investigations and arrests within the city. He had a talent for thief-taking and his services were in demand from private clients, including the Bank of England.

Upon one occasion, when Townsend was to act as escort to a carriage going to Reading, he took with him the famous Joe Manton, the gunmaker, who was always ready for a lark and was as brave as steel. Soon after reaching Hounslow three footpads stopped the coach and Joe Manton was preparing to try the effect of one of his deadly barrels upon them, when Townsend cried out, 'Stop Joe, don't fire! Let me talk to the gentlemen.' The moment the robbers heard Townsend's voice they took to their heels: but he had been able to identify them and a few months afterwards they were taken, tried, and upon Townsend's evidence, sent to Botany Bay.[73]

The short, corpulent police officer was, for his daring exploits and general good conduct, selected by the Home Office to attend at drawing rooms, levees, and all state occasions, and he became a kind of *personage*, and was much noticed by the royal family and the great people of the day.[74] Everyone went up to speak to Townsend. He was eccentric and amusing and somewhat inclined to take advantage of the familiarity with which he was treated, but he was a sort of privileged person and could say what he liked.

On one occasion the Duke of Clarence recommended Townsend to publish his memoirs, which he thought would be very interesting. Townsend, who had become somewhat deaf, seemed rather surprised but said he would obey H. R. H.'s commands. A few weeks afterwards, Townsend was on duty at Carlton House, when the duke asked him if he had fulfilled his promise. His answer was: 'Oh sir, you've got me into a devil of a scrape! I had begun to write my *amours,* as you desired, when Mrs Townsend caught me in the act of writing them and swore she'd be avenged: for you know, your Royal Highness, I was obliged to divulge many secrets about women, for which she'll never forgive me.'

---

73 Townsend was apparently responsible for the first shipment of convicts to Botany Bay, Australia, in 1789.

74 By 1792, Townsend was personally responsible for the security of the royal family, and had become a favourite of the Prince of Wales.

🐾· The Duke Of Wellington And The Author

As everything connected with the Duke of Wellington is received with pleasure by the public, and as what I am going to relate is well-known to many of my contemporaries – who have urged me to put it into print – I am encouraged to relate an anecdote in which I played a prominent part, and which, though it happened forty-five years ago, made so deep an impression on my mind that I can narrate the circumstances as correctly as if they had occurred yesterday.

After leaving the Guards in 1821, I spent some time in Paris, where several of my friends had established themselves and we all pronounced it to be the most delightful city in the world. I remember Luttrell, at a dinner where several alliterative toasts were given – such as London and Liberty, Edinburgh and Education – giving as his toast: Paris and Pocket-money. That most agreeable of men was seldom wrong in anything that he said, and in those days, as we all possessed plenty of the second ingredient of his *sentiment,* we passed a most agreeable time and perhaps lived 'Not wisely but too well'. At all events, we enjoyed ourselves immensely.

In the midst of this very pleasant existence, I happened to call one morning, upon the Princess M__, who lived in the Rue Basse du Rempart. No sooner had we shaken hands than she began speaking of the Duke of Wellington, who had arrived for a few days to see the king and who was then about to leave Paris. She asked me if I was aware that I was no favourite with his Grace, and that he had even spoken of me in no measured terms. I replied that I had not the honour of knowing the duke personally and that my position was too humble a one to attract his notice. 'You are mistaken,' said Madame de M__, 'he has doubtless heard very unfavourable reports of your character, for he has warned young Paul Lieven to beware of forming any intimacy with a man addicted to gambling and the society of opera dancers and actresses, as such an acquaintance might not only lead him astray now, but be very detrimental to his prospects in afterlife.

After hearing this *agreeable* communication, I lost no time in calling on my intimate friend Captain Hesse, a natural son of the Duke of York's, and who at that time was an officer in the 18th Hussars. I related to my *fidus Achates*[75] what had been told me by the Princess and asked his advice as to the line of conduct I ought to pursue.

Hesse, who was personally well known to the duke, offered to call at the English embassy, where his Grace was staying and ask for some explanation of so unwarrantable an attack. Unluckily, the great man had left for London with Lord Fitzroy Somerset that very morning. Hesse and I, therefore, concocted a letter to the duke, in which I entreated his Grace to tell me if the lady's report was correct, as it appeared to me incomprehensible that a person of his exalted station should have thus attacked the private character of a man totally unknown to him.

This letter was duly forwarded to London but did not reach the duke there: for on his arrival in town he had found an invitation from the Prince Regent to pass some days with him at the Pavilion at Brighton, where my letter was placed in his hands. His Grace, with that promptitude for which he was always so remarkable, replied to me in a letter of four pages. I regret that this document – upon which I always placed a high value – is no longer in my hands. I lent it to Count D'Orsay, who was anxious to have a copy of it and notwithstanding that a strict search has been made since his death (amongst the papers that he left behind him, in the possession of his sister, the Duchess de Grammont), I have not been able to recover a document of so much value to me and to society: for it expresses the opinions of a man whose every thought was certain to be respected and well received.

The duke's letter was complimentary to me individually and gave a most dedicated denial of his having uttered any expression that could be considered derogatory to me. He had, he admitted, given some advice to young Count Lieven, but these counsels had no reference to any of his associates. He added that he could not have spoken in such terms of me, as he was totally unacquainted with either my habits or my tastes. To the lady, he never could have mentioned my name, as he had not once been in her society during his short visit to Paris. He had never made any observations about the imprudence or follies of gamblers, for in fact

---

75 'Trusty Achates', i.e. a friend or confidant, as according to Virgil, Achates was a close companion of Aeneas.

some of the best friends he had in the world belonged to that category. He concluded a most dignified letter in his characteristic style by saying that if I was not fully convinced of his not deserving the imputation that had been cast upon him of abusing me, he was perfectly ready to give me any satisfaction that I might think proper to demand.[76]

I cannot call to mind – even at the distance of time – the noble conduct of the great duke on this occasion without feeling deeply affected.

Throughout the whole of his eventful career, the Duke of Wellington always placed first and foremost, far above his military and social honours, his position as an English gentleman. How few in his Grace's exalted station would have condescended even to notice such a letter as mine, worded though it was in a most respectful manner, or have deigned to give so full and ample an explanation. And how few would, like that truly great man, have waved their high military rank in a discussion with an obscure subaltern and declared themselves ready to give him redress *sur le champ*, if he still considered himself injured and aggrieved.

I am proud to think that the great duke did not bear malice or think any the worse of me for the explanation I had demanded. In the year 1824, I happened to be walking one morning in the Park near Apsley House with my friend Charles, commonly called Cornet Wortley. We had not been there long when we met the duke, who called Wortley to him and after a short conversation, as I stood on one side, I heard him ask Wortley who I was, and on his answering, as I took off my hat the duke smiled, touched his, and nodded to me most good-naturedly several times.

⚞· Coronation Of George IV

At this gorgeous solemnity it fell to my lot to be on guard on the platform

---

76 Wellington's attitude towards duelling was inconsistent: he frequently maintained that he disapproved of the practice, and had declined to meet the son of Marshal Ney, who had accused him of withholding influence over Louis XVIII in 1815, thus abandoning his father to a Bourbon firing squad; yet had felt himself obliged to meet Lord Winchilsea on 21st March 1828, in order to defend his support for Catholic Emancipation – though in the event, both men deliberately fired wide.

along which the royal procession had to pass, in order to reach the Abbey. The crowd that had congregated in this locality exceeded anything I had ever before seen: struggling, fighting, shrieking, and laughing, were the order of the day among this motley assemblage. Little Townsend, the chief police officer of Bow Street, with his flaxen wig and broad-brimmed hat, was to be seen hurrying from one end of the platform to the other, assuming immense importance. On the approach of the *cortège* you heard this officious person, 'Dressed with a little brief authority', hallooing with all his might: 'Gentlemen and ladies, take care of your pockets for you are surrounded by thieves!' and hearty laughter responded to Mr Townsend's salutary advice.

When the procession was seen to approach and the royal canopy came in sight, those below the platform were straining with all their might to get a peep at the sovereign and the confusion at this moment can be better imagined than described. The pickpockets, of course, had availed themselves of the confusion, and in the twinkling of an eye there were more watches and purses snatched from the pockets of His Majesty's loyal subjects than perhaps on any other occasion.

Amidst the crowd a respectable gentleman from the Principality [Wales] hallooed out in his provincial tongue: 'Mr Townsend! Mr Townsend! I have been robbed of my gold watch and purse containing all my money. What am I to do? What am I to do to get home? I have come 200 miles to see this sight and instead of receiving satisfaction or hospitality, I am robbed by those cut-throats called the Swell Mob.' This eloquent speech had a very different effect upon the mob than the poor Welshman had reason to expect: for all of a sudden the refrain of the song of *Sweet Home* was shouted by a thousand voices, and the mob bawled out, 'Go back to your goats, my good fellow!' The indignities that were heaped upon this unfortunate gentleman during the royal procession – and his appearance after the king had passed – created pity in the minds of all honest persons who witnessed this disgusting scene: his hat was beaten over his eyes and his coat, neckcloth, etc., were torn off his body. For there were no police in those days, and with the exception of a few constables and some soldiers, there was no force to prevent the metropolis from being burned to the ground, if it had pleased the mob to set it on fire.[77]

⟩⟨· Ladies' Jewellery And Lovers

Some of the most magnificent fortunes in England have, in the first instance, been undermined by an extravagant expenditure on jewellery, which has been given to ladies – married and unmarried – who have fascinated their wealthy admirers and made them their slaves. Hamlet, Rundell, and Bridge were in my day patronised by the great and obtained large sums of money from their enamoured clients, to whom they often became bankers.

On the coronation of George IV, Hamlet made his appearance at the house of Mr Coutts,[78] in Piccadilly, on the corner of Stratton Street. It was during dinner but owing, no doubt, to a previous arrangement, he was at once admitted, when he placed before the rich banker a magnificent diamond cross, which had been worn the day before by the Duke of York. It at once attracted the admiration of Mrs Coutts,[79] who loudly exclaimed: 'How happy I should be with such a splendid specimen of jewellery!' 'What is it worth?' immediately exclaimed Mr Coutts. 'I could not allow it to pass out of my possession for less than £15,000,' said the wary tradesman. 'Bring me a pen and ink,' was the only answer made by

---

77 The coronation of George IV took place at Westminster Abbey on 19th July 1821. Despite the unwelcome arrival of his estranged wife, Caroline – who was barred from entry on his orders, and turned away by prizefighters dressed as pages – George enjoyed his big day. Swamped in ceremonial robes, including a train twenty-seven feet long, and wearing a crown containing 12,314 diamonds, George spent much of the five-hour ceremony winking, sighing, and making eyes at his mistress, Lady Conyngham. But afterwards, returning in his carriage to Carlton House, George found the road blocked by several overturned coaches, and fearful of mob mischief, instructed his driver to take him home by back roads.

78 Thomas Coutts (1735–1822), the king's banker.

79 Harriot Mellon (1777–1837), an actress whom Coutts secretly married in January 1815, on the death of his first wife, Susannah Starkie, who had been mentally ill for some time. Coutts married Harriot in public on 12th April 1815.

the doting husband, and he at once drew a cheque for that amount from the bank in the Strand, and with much delight the worthy old gentleman placed the jewel upon the fair bosom of the lady.

The Earl of C__, whose reputation in the sporting world was one of the highest order and who had obtained some notoriety by his amours, fell into the hands of Hamlet, who was known to the aristocracy by his mock-title of Prince of Denmark. Hamlet placed before him on one occasion jewels to the amount of £30,000 and volunteered – as his client was not of age – to give him credit for several months. The offer was accepted and the brilliant present became the possession of a young lady, Mademoiselle G__, one of the Terpsichorean tribe, whose charms had captivated the youthful nobleman. She had irrevocably fascinated him by the expression of her love, awakened by the prospect of a rich remuneration, and she accepted him as the sole possessor of a heart that had been before at the disposal of any rich admirer whose purse was worthy of her consideration.

This lady, who is now somewhat advanced in years but has still the remains of beauty, is living in France upon her estate: the produce of the many charms that she once possessed, and which she turned to such advantage as to make her society, even up to this day, courted by those who look upon wealth as the great source of distinction, and who are willing to disbelieve any stories they may accidentally hear of her previous history.

〜• Crockford's Club

I have alluded to the high play which took place at White's and Brookes's in the olden time, and at Wattier's in the days of Brummell and the Dandies. Charles Fox, George Selwyn, Lord Carlisle, Fitzpatrick, Horace Walpole, the Duke of Queensberry, and others, lost whole fortunes at faro, macao, and hazard. Almost the only winners, indeed, of that generation were General Scott, father-in-law of Canning, the Duke of Portland, and Lord Robert Spencer – Lord Robert, indeed, bought the beautiful estate of Woolbidding, in Sussex with the proceeds of his gains by keeping the bank at Brookes's.

But in the reign of George IV a new star rose upon the horizon in the person of Mr William Crockford[80] and the old fashioned games of faro, macao, and lansquenet gave way to the all-devouring thirst for the game of hazard. Crockey, when still a young man, had relinquished the peaceful trade of a fishmonger[81] for a share in a 'hell' where, with his partner, Gye, he managed to win – after a sitting of twenty-four hours – the enormous sum of £100,000 from Lords Thanet and Granville, Mr Ball Hughes, and two other gentlemen whose names I do not now remember. With this capital added to his former gains, he built the well-known palace in St James's Street, where a club was established and play organised on a scale of magnificence and liberality hitherto unknown in Europe.[82]

One may sagely say without exaggeration that Crockford won the whole of the ready money of the then existing generation. As is often the case at Lords Cricket ground, the great match of the gentlemen of England against the professional players, was won by the latter. It was a very hollow thing and in a few years £1,200,000 was swept away by the fortunate fishmonger. He did not, however, die worth more than a sixth part of this vast sum: the difference being swallowed up in various unlucky speculations.

No one can describe the splendour and excitement of the early days of Crockey. A supper of the most exquisite kind, prepared by the famous Ude,[83] and accompanied by the best wines in the world, together with every luxury of the season, was furnished *gratis*. The members of the club included all the celebrities of England, from the Duke of Wellington to the youngest ensign of the Guards, and at the glad and festive board,

---

80 Baptized in 1776, died in 1844.

81 Barely literate at this time, Crockford never lost his cockney accent.

82 Crockford opened the doors of his club at 50 St James's Street – a row of four houses, in fact, which had been turned into a 'palace of gambling' – in 1828, limiting the club's membership to 1,200 persons.

83 Louis-Eustache Ude (died 1846), formerly a chef at the court of Louis XVI, reputedly fled to London from revolutionary Paris. By the 1820s, however, Ude was a celebrity and his employment by Crockford (at the unheard of sum of £4,000 per annum) was a coup, which added caché to his new establishment. A temperamental culinary genius with an explosive temper, Ude quit Crockfords in 1838 after a fight with the management.

which was constantly replenished from midnight to early dawn – the most brilliant sallies of wit, the most agreeable conversation, the most interesting anecdotes (interspersed with grave political discussions and acute logical reasoning on every conceivable subject) proceeded from the soldiers, scholars, statesmen, poets, and men of pleasure, who, when the house was up and balls and parties at an end, delighted to finish their evening with a little supper and a good deal of hazard at old Crockey's. The tone of the club was excellent. A most gentlemanlike feeling prevailed and none of the rudeness, familiarity, and ill-breeding that disgrace some of the minor clubs of the present day would have been tolerated for a moment.

Though not many years have elapsed since the time of which I write, the supper table had a very different appearance from what it would present did the club now exist. Beards were completely unknown and the rare mustachios were only worn by officers of the Household Brigade or hussar regiments. Stiff white neckcloths, blue coats and brass buttons, rather short-waisted white waistcoats, and tremendously embroidered shirt fronts with gorgeous studs of great value, were considered the right thing. A late deservedly popular colonel in the Guards used to give Storr and Mortimer £25 a year to furnish him with a new set of studs every Saturday night during the London season.

The great foreign diplomatists, Prince Talleyrand, Count Pozzo di Borgo, General Alava, the Duke of Palmella, Prince Esterhazy, the French, Russian, Spanish, Portuguese, and Austrian ambassadors, and all persons of distinction and eminence who arrived in England, belonged to Crockford's as a matter of course, but many rued the day when they became members of that fascinating but dangerous *coterie*. The great duke himself – always rather a friend of the dandies – did not disdain to appear now and then at this charming club, whilst the late Lord Raglan, Lord Anglesey, Sir Hussey Vivian, and many more of our Peninsular and Waterloo heroes, were constant visitors. The two great novelists of the day, who have since become great statesmen, Disraeli and Bulwer Lytton, displayed at that brilliant supper table the one his sable, the other his auburn curls. There, Horace Twiss made proof of an appetite, and Edward

Montague of a thirst, which astonished all beholders. Whilst the bitter jests of Sir Joseph Copley, Colonel Armstrong, and John Wilson Croker, and the brilliant wit of Alvanley, were the delight of all present, and their *bon mots* were the next day retailed all over England.

In the playroom might be heard the clear ringing voice of that agreeable reprobate, Tom Duncombe, as he cheerfully called, 'Seven!' and the powerful hand of the vigorous Sefton in throwing for a ten. There might be noted the scientific dribbling of a four by 'King' Allen, the tremendous backing of nines and fives by Ball Hughes and Auriol, the enormous stakes played for by Lords Lichfield and Chesterfield, George Payne, Sir Vincent Cotton, D'Orsay, and George Anson: and above all, the gentlemanly bearing and calm and unmoved demeanour, under losses or gains, of all the men of that generation.

The old fishmonger himself, seated snug and sly at his desk in the corner of the room, watchful as the dragon that guarded the golden apples of Hesperides, would only give credit to sure and approved signatures. Who that ever entered that dangerous little room can ever forget the large green table with the croupiers, Page, Darking, and Bacon, with their suave manners, sleek appearance, stiff white neckcloths, and the almost miraculous quickness and dexterity with which they swept away the money of the unfortunate punters when the fatal cry of 'Deuce ace!' 'Aces!' or 'Sixes out!' was heard in answer to the caster's bold cry of 'Seven!' or 'Nine!' or 'Five's the main!'

O noctes cœnœque deûm![84] But the brightest medal has its reverse, and after all the wit and gaiety and excitement of the night, how disagreeable the waking up, and how very unpleasant the sight of the little card, with its numerous figures marked down on the debtor side in the fine bold hand of Mr Page. Alas, poor Crockey's! Shorn of its former glory, has become a sort of refuge for the destitute: a cheap dining-house.[85] How are the mighty

---

84 'Oh nights and suppers of the gods' from Horace's *Satires*.

85 After Crockford's death in 1844 his premises were sold, becoming the Naval, Military, and Civil Service Club; then a restaurant, the 'Wellington'; then an auction room; then the offices of a hotel company; then, in 1874, the Devonshire Club.

fallen! Irish buckeens [bullies], spring captains, welchers [someone who evades paying a debt] from Newmarket, and suspicious-looking foreigners, may be seen swaggering after dinner, through the marble halls and up that gorgeous staircase where once the chivalry of England loved to congregate. And those who remember Crockford's in all its glory, cast as they pass, a look of unavailing regret at its dingy walls with many a sigh to the memory of the pleasant days they passed there, and the companions and noble gentlemen who have long since gone to their last home.

⚞ Then And Now

Perhaps it is because I am growing old, and woman has less power to charm than heretofore; but, whatever may be the reason, I cannot help thinking that, in 'the merry days when I was young', or 'in my hot youth, when George the Third was king', the women of England were more beautiful, better bred, and more distinguished in appearance – and above all, in manner – than they are now-a-days. How grand they used to look with their tall, stately forms, small, thoroughbred heads, and long, flowing ringlets: dreamlike fair and queenly as Ossian's fabled daughters! You could not help feeling somewhat elated and self-satisfied, if perchance one of those sidelong glances – half-proud, half-bashful, like a petted child's – fell upon you, leaving you silent and pensive, full of hopes and memories. Egad! it was worth being loved by such women as those! And if there were then, as now, tales of sin and shame, there were also the extenuating circumstances of strong temptation, overwhelming passion, self-sacrifice, remorse: often the blighted heart and early grave – things almost unknown in these days of flirtation and frivolity.

I do not mean to say that there are not now, as there always have been in every state of society, beautiful and amiable women, combining good sense and high principle: but there are too many who seem to have taken for their ideal a something between the dashing London horse-breaker and some Parisian *artiste dramatique* of a third-rate theatre; the object of whose ambition is to be mistaken for a *femme du demi-monde,* to be insulted when they walk out with their petticoats girt up to their knees, showing (to do them justice) remarkably pretty feet and legs, and to wearing wide-awake hats over painted cheeks and brows, and walk with that indescribable, jaunty, 'devil-may-care' look which is considered 'the right thing' now-a-days; to make sporting bets; to address men as Jack, Tom, or Harry; to ride ahead in the Park [i.e. in front of the men in St James's Park]; to call the paterfamilias 'governor' and the lady mother 'the old party'; to talk of the young men who 'spoon' them [i.e. to make silly shows of affection], and discuss with them the merits of 'Skittles' and her horses, or the last scandalous story fabricated in the bay window at White's, the very faintest allusion to which would have made their mothers' hair stand on end with dismay and horror: this is to be pleasant and 'fast' [immoral] and amusing. The young lady, who is weak enough to blush if addressed rather too familiarly, and so unwise as to ignore the existence of *les dames aux camelias*[86] is called 'slow' [dull] and distanced altogether: in the London steeplechase after husbands she is 'nowhere' – an outsider – a female muff [awkward]. The girl of the year 1862 who is not 'fast' is generally dull and *blasée,* pleased with nothing, and possesses neither the wisdom of age nor the *naïveté* of youth.

I have often heard discussions on the comparative degrees of worldliness in London and Parisian society. It has been my lot in my day to mingle much in both, and I should be inclined to bestow the palm for frivolity on our volatile neighbours the French, and adjudge to my own countrywomen that of worldliness. In Paris, the atmosphere is light, clear, and brilliant, conversation free and easy, and the people really love pleasure for pleasure's sake. From the dapper little *grisette* [a young Frenchwoman of the lower classes] in her neat calico gown and tidy cap, who accompanies her favourite *étudiant* [student] Leon Lionceau to the Closerie des Lilac, and winds up with cold veal, salad, and beer, at six in the morning, in her beloved's garret on the sixth storey, to the high-bred comtesse, who, after a round of balls, 'comes to champagne and a chicken at last' at the Maison Dorée with that magnificent dandy, Arthur de Crèvecoeur, it is all

---

86 A reference to Dumas' novel, *La Dame aux Camelias*, whose heroine, Marguerite Gaultier, is a notoriously beautiful and alluring courtesan with very expensive tastes.

the same mad, and, to a certain degree, successful hunt after amusement. *Vive le plaisir!* is the cry of the Parisian population. They invoke it, and it does come; they grasp the shadow of it as it flies rapidly along; and they would sell the soul (of whose existence they doubt) for that day of pleasure in which they fully believe. As far as they can manage it, they strive to make life one joyous holiday.

Now the good Londoners do not seem as if they expected to be amused. As Froissart said of them 500 years ago, 'they take their pleasure sadly,' with long faces and lugubrious voices, set to a particular whining tone. Mrs Danby Tremayne comes up for the London season, hires a house in Lower Grosvenor Street, very dark, very dirty, very dear, and nurtures in her expansive bosom the stern determination 'to go everywhere' – that is, within the range of the charmed circle of good society. Mrs Danby Tremayne would be unspeakably wretched if her name – and those of all her daughters who have been presented – did not figure in the columns of the *Morning Post.* In spite of her antiquated notions concerning the propriety of deportment and modesty of speech becoming youthful maidens, she would force those shy, demure, straight-laced, red-elbowed damsels, to frisk about, talk slang, and wear wide-awakes, and praise Anonyma, if by these means she could get an invitation to __ House, or see the faintest chance of capturing some fast young lord.

Amelia, Countess of Crinoline – who is on the wrong side of fifty – is worn to a shadow in running after what is called pleasure. She considers herself in duty bound to show her poor hollow cheeks and skinny shoulders everywhere, lest it should be said that she is voted an 'old party' and only asked to 'rococo' drums. That worn out, painted old harridan, Lady Rattlesnake, whose daughters – ay, and grand-daughters too – are all married and going their melancholy rounds on their own account, takes possession of some handsome, but friendless damsel, and uses her as a decoy to obtain invitations and an arm to lean upon and throw her cloak over her gaunt shoulders. And woe betide the poor dependent girl if the expected civilities are wanting, and the good-looking young guardsman, who delights to gaze into Isabella's bright eyes and whisper soft nonsense in her ear, should rebel at finding himself compelled to make the agreeable and give his arm to the withered old mummy, call her carriage, etc., etc. Should he take himself off, muttering, 'This won't pay.' the ancient dowager on her way home snubs poor Isabella, accuses her of being slow, stupid, unattractive, and so on: and the wretched girl, as she throws her beautiful head wearily back on the cushions, murmurs to herself, echoing the devil's whisper, 'I have not been fast enough to please him this evening, but tomorrow he will hand out Lady Rattlesnake with all the ardour of a youthful lover.'

In London in bygone days a worldly man or woman would, without scruple, cut their father or mother did they not belong to the particular set which they considered good society. Mr S __ was once riding in the Park many years ago with the Marquis of C __, then one of the kings of the fashionable world, and some other dandies of that day, when they met a respectable-looking elderly man, who nodded somewhat familiarly to S __ . 'Who's your friend?' drawled Lord C __. 'That?' replied S __, 'oh, a very good sort of a fellow, one of my Cheshire farmers.' It was his own father: a most amiable and excellent man, and who had better blood in his veins, and a larger fortune, than any of the lordlings by whom his unworthy son was surrounded. A celebrated leader of fashion, Lady X __, never asked her own mother, a well-born and well-conducted, but somewhat eccentric person, to any of her parties: she ignored her very existence, and yet she was by nature a kind, well-meaning, and good-natured woman. But the world's canker had eaten into her heart.

In these days of railways and monster parties, the folly of exclusiveness has very much died away. Cutting near relatives is out of fashion: it is unnecessary in the whirl and bustle of life. There is little chance of meeting those we do not seek, and there is more self-respect among those who do not belong to the upper ten thousand. Jones does not care one straw whether young Lord Popinjay cuts him or not. He has his own circle of admirers – his own particular summer and winter toady. He is a much better-looking fellow, and while Popinjay is sending Perdita or Imogen Kettledrum enormous bouquets, and catching cold under her window, the handsome Jones is snugly ensconced in the lady's boudoir, eating pigeon pie and mimicking the unlucky lord. Miss Jackson, if a pretty girl, a good dancer, and showy rider, will have more partners and invitations than Lady Araminta Drystick, with her ancient pedigree and aristocratic airs.

How unspeakably odious – with a few brilliant exceptions, such as Alvanley and others – were the dandies of forty years ago. They were a motley crew, with nothing remarkable about them but their insolence. They were generally not high-born, nor rich, nor very good-looking, nor clever, nor agreeable; and why they arrogated to themselves the right of setting up their own fancied superiority on a self-raised pedestal, and despising their betters, Heaven only knows. They were generally middle-aged, some even elderly men, had large appetites and weak digestions, gambled freely – and had no luck. They hated everybody, and abused everybody, and would sit together in White's bay window, or the pit boxes at the Opera, weaving tremendous crammers. They swore a good deal, never laughed, had their own particular slang, looked hazy after dinner, and had most of them been patronised at one time or other by Brummell and the Prince Regent. These gentlemen were very fond of having a butt. Many years ago Tom Raikes[87] filled this capacity: though he did kick out sometimes, and to some purpose. They gloried in their shame, and believed in nothing good, or noble, or elevated. Thank Heaven, that miserable race of used-up dandies has long been extinct! May England never look upon their like again!

⋙ • ⋘

---

87 Thomas Raikes (1777–1848), dandy and diarist.